LAW, CRIME AND LAW ENFORCEMENT

RISK ASSESSMENT AND SENTENCING IN THE CRIMINAL JUSTICE SYSTEM

CONSIDERATIONS AND PROPOSALS

LAW, CRIME AND LAW ENFORCEMENT

Additional books in this series can be found on Nova's website under the Series tab.

Additional e-books in this series can be found on Nova's website under the e-book tab.

LAW, CRIME AND LAW ENFORCEMENT

RISK ASSESSMENT AND SENTENCING IN THE CRIMINAL JUSTICE SYSTEM

CONSIDERATIONS AND PROPOSALS

JULIA CAMPBELL
EDITOR

nova publishers
New York

Library of Congress Cataloging-in-Publication Data

ISBN: 978-1-63484-561-8

Published by Nova Science Publishers, Inc. † New York

CONTENTS

PREFACE

The number of people incarcerated in the United States has increased significantly over the past three decades from approximately 419,000 inmates in 1983 to approximately 1.5 million inmates in 2013. Concerns about both the economic and social consequences of the country's growing reliance on incarceration have led to calls for reforms to the nation's criminal justice system. There have been legislative proposals to implement a risk and needs assessment system in federal prisons. The system would be used to place inmates in rehabilitative programs. Under the proposed system some inmates would be eligible to earn additional time credits for participating in rehabilitative programs that reduce their risk of recidivism. Such credits would allow inmates to be placed on prerelease custody earlier. The proposed system would exclude inmates convicted of certain offenses from being eligible to earn additional time credits. This book provides information on the use of risk and needs assessment in the criminal justice system. It starts with an overview of risk and needs assessment and a discussion of some of the critiques of it, and also discusses issues policymakers might consider if they debate legislation to expand the use of risk and needs assessment in the federal prison system. Moreover, the book reviews mandatory minimum sentencing legislation in the 114th Congress.

In: Risk Assessment and Sentencing …
Editor: Julia Campbell
ISBN: 978-1-63484-561-8

Chapter 1

RISK AND NEEDS ASSESSMENT IN THE CRIMINAL JUSTICE SYSTEM*

Nathan James

SUMMARY

The number of people incarcerated in the United States has increased significantly over the past three decades from approximately 419,000 inmates in 1983 to approximately 1.5 million inmates in 2013. Concerns about both the economic and social consequences of the country's growing reliance on incarceration have led to calls for reforms to the nation's criminal justice system.

There have been legislative proposals to implement a risk and needs assessment system in federal prisons. The system would be used to place inmates in rehabilitative programs. Under the proposed system some inmates would be eligible to earn additional time credits for participating in rehabilitative programs that reduce their risk of recidivism. Such credits would allow inmates to be placed on prerelease custody earlier. The proposed system would exclude inmates convicted of certain offenses from being eligible to earn additional time credits.

Risk and needs assessment instruments typically consist of a series of items used to collect data on behaviors and attitudes that research indicates are related to the risk of recidivism. Generally, inmates are

* This is an edited, reformatted and augmented version of a Congressional Research Service publication R44087, prepared for Members and Committees of Congress, dated October 13, 2015.

classified as being high, moderate, or low risk. Assessment instruments are comprised of static and dynamic risk factors. Static risk factors do not change, while dynamic risk factors can either change on their own or be changed through an intervention. In general, research suggests that the most commonly used assessment instruments can, with a moderate level of accuracy, predict who is at risk for violent recidivism. It also suggests that no single instrument is superior to any other when it comes to predictive validity.

The Risk-Needs-Responsivity (RNR) model has become the dominant paradigm in risk and needs assessment. The risk principle states that high-risk offenders need to be placed in programs that provide more intensive treatment and services while low-risk offenders should receive minimal or even no intervention. The need principle states that effective treatment should focus on addressing needs that contribute to criminal behavior. The responsivity principle states that rehabilitative programming should be delivered in a style and mode that is consistent with the ability and learning style of the offender.

However, the wide-scale adoption of risk and needs assessment in the criminal justice system is not without controversy. Several critiques have been raised against the use of risk and needs assessment, including that it could have discriminatory effects because some risk factors are correlated with race; that it uses group base rates for recidivism to make determinations about an individual's propensity for re-offending; and that risk and needs assessment are two distinct procedures and should be conducted separately.

There are several issues policymakers might contemplate should Congress choose to consider legislation to implement a risk and needs assessment system in federal prisons, including the following:

- Should risk and needs assessment be used in federal prisons?
- Should certain inmates be excluded from earning additional time credits?
- Should risk assessment be incorporated into sentencing?
- Should there be a decreased focus on punishing offenders?

The number of people incarcerated in the United States has increased dramatically over the past three decades. In 1983, there were approximately 419,000 inmates under the jurisdiction of state and federal correctional authorities.[1] By the end of 2013, this figure reached approximately 1.5 million inmates.[2] The incarceration rate increased from 179 per 100,000 people in 1983 to 478 per 100,000 in 2013. While research indicates that the expanded use of incarceration during the 1980s and 1990s did contribute to the declining crime rate, the effect was likely small,[3] and incarceration has probably reached the point of diminishing returns.[4] Concerns about both the economic and social consequences of the country's burgeoning prison population have resulted in organizations such as Right on Crime and the Coalition for Public Safety calling for reforms to the nation's criminal justice system. Congress also formed the Charles Colson Task Force on Federal Corrections to examine the growth of the federal prison population and provide recommendations for reforms.[5]

There are two, not mutually exclusive, methods to reduce the number of incarcerated individuals in the United States: send fewer people to prison (e.g., placing offenders on probation or in a diversion program like a drug court) and/or release more inmates (e.g., placing inmates on parole or granting them early release by allowing them to earn more good time credits). While the ideas of diverting "low-level drug offenders" from prison or granting non-violent offenders early release so they can serve a greater proportion of their sentence in the community have been popular proposals to reduce the prison population, the crime someone is convicted of is not always the best proxy for the risk that person might pose to the community. For example, people who might not be violent individuals and who pose a low risk for future violence might be convicted of, what are legally defined as, violent crimes (e.g., illegal gun possession or driving the get-away car for someone who committed an armed robbery).[6] On the other hand, violent people might be sentenced to prison for non-violent crimes as a result of a plea deal.[7]

Because courts and correctional officials make decisions about who can safely be diverted from incarceration or granted early release, they may benefit from tools that can help in this process. Actuarial risk assessment tools may serve this purpose. Needs assessments could also help correctional officials make determinations about which offenders need higher levels of supervision and/or rehabilitative programming. Assessment instruments might help increase the efficiency of the criminal justice system by identifying low-risk offenders who could be effectively managed on probation rather than incarcerated, and they might help identify high-risk offenders who would gain the most by being placed in rehabilitative programs.

The use of risk and needs assessment in the criminal justice system is not without controversy, however. Proponents of assessment assert that the tools used to assess the risk and needs of inmates are better than the independent judgment of clinicians and that the tools have demonstrated the ability to make distinctions between high- and low-risk offenders.[8] Nonetheless, risk and needs assessment is not 100% accurate. Two experts in the field note that "[a]lthough statistical risk assessment reduces uncertainty about an offender's probable future conduct, it is subject to errors and should be regarded as advisory rather than peremptory. Even with large data sets and advanced analytical techniques, the best models are usually able to predict recidivism with about 70% accuracy—provided it is completed by trained staff."[9]

There have been legislative proposals introduced in the current Congress that would require the Bureau of Prisons (BOP) to implement a risk and needs assessment system.[10] The system would evaluate inmates and place inmates in rehabilitative programs and productive activities. Under the proposed system some inmates would be allowed to earn additional time credits for participating in rehabilitative programs that reduce their risk of recidivism. Such credits would allow inmates to be placed in prerelease custody earlier.

This report provides information on the use of risk and needs assessment in the criminal justice system. It starts with an overview of risk and needs assessment and a discussion of some of the critiques of it. The report concludes with a discussion of the issues policymakers might consider if they debate legislation to expand the use of risk and needs assessment in the federal prison system.

An Overview of Risk and Needs Assessment

A risk and needs assessment instrument measures offenders' criminal risk factors and specific needs that if addressed will reduce the likelihood of future criminal activity.[11] Assessment instruments typically consist of a series of questions that help guide an interview with an offender in order to collect data on behaviors and attitudes that research indicates are related to the risk of recidivism.[12] Data collected during the interview is typically supplemented with information from an official records check, such as a criminal history records check.[13] A total score is calculated using the risk and needs assessment instrument, and that score places the offender into a risk category (typically "low," "moderate," or "high").

Risk and Needs Factors

Generally speaking, risk and needs assessment instruments typically consist of both static and dynamic risk factors. Static risk factors do not change over time. Examples include age at first arrest, gender, past problems with substance or alcohol abuse, prior mental health problems, or a past history of violating terms of supervision (e.g., parole or probation).[14]

Dynamic risk factors, also called "criminogenic[15] needs," change and/or can be addressed through interventions. Examples include current age, education level, or marital status; being currently employed or in substance or alcohol abuse treatment; and having a stable residence.[16]

Can Risk and Needs Assessment Instruments Accurately Predict Risk?

In general, research indicates that most commonly used risk and needs assessment instruments can, with a moderate level of accuracy, predict who is at risk for recidivism.[17] It also indicates that no one instrument is superior to any other when it comes to predictive validity.[18] One group of researchers concluded that "[o]verall, our results showed that all of the nine tools predicted violence at above-chance levels, with medium effect sizes, and no one tool predicting violence significantly better than any other. In sum, all did well, but none came first."[19]

The relative interchangeability of risk and needs assessment instruments was demonstrated by an experiment whereby items from four instruments were written on pieces of paper and placed in a coffee can, and researchers drew 13 of the items from the coffee can at random to create four new instruments. The researchers found that the four "coffee can" instruments predicted violent recidivism as well as the four original needs and risk assessment instruments.[20]

Two scholars have posited that there might be two explanations for why well-validated risk and needs assessment instruments have similar levels of performance. First, some evidence suggests that there is a "natural limit" to the predictive utility of instruments.[21] Simply stated, there is a limit to how accurately recidivism can be predicted given society's current level of knowledge about criminal behavior. Second, well-validated instruments may show similar levels of performance because they are tapping "common factors" or shared dimensions of risk, even though the instruments utilize different items or have different approaches.[22] For example, the researchers who conducted the "coffee can" experiment found that assessment instruments gauge four overlapping dimensions: criminal history, persistent antisocial lifestyle, psychopathic personality, and alcohol/mental health issues.

How Risk and Needs Assessment Is Used in the Criminal Justice System

Risk and needs assessment can be used at nearly all points of the criminal justice system, as highlighted by a Vera Institute of Justice memorandum.[23]

- *Pretrial detention:* Courts use risk assessment instruments to help them make decisions about which defendants can be safely released pending trial. The assessment typically measures the likelihood the defendant will appear if released and whether the defendant is likely to commit another offense while on release.
- *Sentencing:* Risk and needs assessment can be used to help a sentencing judge decide whether an offender should be incarcerated or placed on community supervision. The result of the assessment can also help the judge decide whether any conditions should be placed on the offender.
- *Probation/Post-Release Supervision:* Probation and parole agents use risk and needs assessment instruments to predict the likelihood that offenders will recidivate and to identify offenders' criminogenic needs. The results of the assessment help probation and parole agents make decisions about (1) the level of supervision offenders will receive, (2) developing an individualized case management plan that focuses on placing offenders in programs that help reduce their risk of recidivism; and (3) sanctions for violations of the conditions of release.
- *Prison:* Correctional authorities use risk assessment to make decisions about the security level to which inmates will be assigned (e.g., a high, medium, low, or minimum security facility). Prison classification systems traditionally try to identify inmates who are at a high risk for escaping or who might be management problems.
- *Parole Boards and Releasing Authorities:* Risk assessment can be used by parole boards and releasing authorities to make decisions about which inmates can be safely released from incarceration.

Two experts on the use of risk and needs assessment note that while there is evidence that risk and needs assessment is widely used in corrections, there is a great deal of variation in how it is implemented and employed.[24] Some states have adopted and implemented standardized assessment instruments that are used throughout the state and across a wide variety of settings.[25] Other states use risk and needs assessment in a less systematic manner.

An Example of Risk and Needs Assessment from Ohio

The Ohio Risk Assessment System (ORAS) provides an example of how risk and needs assessment can be integrated into the criminal justice system. Ohio passed a law that required the Ohio Department of Rehabilitation and Corrections to develop a risk assessment tool to evaluate the likelihood of recidivism for adult offenders.[26] The law required the risk assessment tool to be used by

- each municipal, county, and common pleas court, when it orders an assessment for sentencing or other purposes,
- the probation department serving those courts,
- state and local correctional institutions,
- private correctional institutions,
- community-based correctional facilities, and
- the Adult Parole Authority and the Ohio Parole Board.

ORAS was "developed as a statewide system to assess the risk and needs of Ohio offenders in order to improve consistency and facilitate communication across criminal justice agencies."27 The goal was to develop assessment tools that were predictive of recidivism at different stages in the criminal justice system; specifically, pretrial release, community supervision, prison intake, and community reentry. The ORAS consists of seven different tools that are used at various points in the criminal justice system:

- the Pre-Trial Tool (PAT),
- the Community Supervision Screening Tool (CSST),
- the Community Supervision Tool (CST),
- the Prison Screening Tool (PST),
- the Prison Intake Tool (PIT),
- the Reentry Tool (RT), and
- the Supplemental Reentry Tool (SRT)

Ohio is highlighted as a noteworthy example because the state developed a statewide risk and needs assessment system that is used across all levels of its correctional system.

Risk-Needs-Responsivity (RNR) Principles

The Risk-Needs-Responsivity (RNR) model of risk and needs assessment and offender treatment incorporates many of the evidence-based practices for reducing recidivism.[28] As the name implies, the model has three main principles: assessing risk, addressing criminogenic needs, and providing treatment that is responsive to the offender's abilities and learning style.[29]

The RNR model is based on the social psychology of offending, which posits that individuals and social/situational factors intersect to create values, cognitions, and personality orientations that are conducive to criminal conduct.[30] These ways of thinking and responding are learned and become reinforced through feedback, and they eventually result in individual differences in the propensity for criminal behavior.[31] The RNR model has become a dominant paradigm in the assessment literature because it is one of the few comprehensive theories of how to provide effective intervention to offenders. Experts in the field of risk and needs assessment assert that assessment systems should adhere to the RNR model. As the Vera Institute of Justice notes, "[u]nderlying the development of evidence-based practices in the criminal justice system are the *risk*, *need*, and *responsivity* principles" [emphasis original].[32]

Many other theories of criminal behavior focus on the social causes of criminal behavior, factors that cannot be addressed through treatment. On the other hand, the RNR model focuses on the proximate causes of criminal behavior, which can be the focus of effective correctional treatment.

Risk Principle

The risk principle has two aspects: (1) criminal behavior can be predicted, and (2) the level of treatment should be matched to the risk level of the offender.[33] The risk principle states that high-risk offenders need to be placed in programs that provide more intensive treatment and services while low-risk offenders should receive minimal or even no intervention.

Needs Principle

The needs principle states that effective treatment should focus on addressing criminogenic needs, that is, dynamic risk factors that are highly correlated with criminal conduct.[34] Also, according to the needs principle, effective treatment should not focus on addressing noncriminogenic needs, because changes in noncriminogenic needs are not associated with reduced recidivism.[35]

Responsivity Principle

The responsivity principle states that rehabilitative programming should be delivered in a style and mode that is consistent with the ability and learning style of the offender.[36] The responsivity principle is further divided into two elements. The general responsivity principle states that cognitive-behavioral and social learning therapies are the most effective form of intervention.[37] The specific responsivity principle states that treatment should consider the relevant characteristics of the offender (e.g., the offender's motivations, preferences, personality, age, gender, ethnicity, and cultural identification, along with other factors).

"Central Eight" Risk and Needs Factors

The developers of the RNR principles identified what they deem the "central eight" risk and needs factors. These risk and needs factors include the "big four," which they believe to be the "major predictor variables and indeed the major causal variable in the analysis of criminal behavior in individuals."[38] The remaining four risk and needs factors are referred to as the "moderate four." The "central eight" risk and needs factors are presented in *Table 1*.

Even though antisocial behavior is the most prominent of the "central eight" risk and needs factors, a common mistake in risk assessment is conflating past antisocial behavior with current antisocial behavior. The seriousness of the current offense is *not* a risk factor.[39] A past history of antisocial behavior is what indicates a risk of future offending.

Table 1. Major Risk and Needs Factors: The "Central Eight"

Risk/Need Factor	Indicator	Target for Intervention
	The Big Four	
History of Antisocial Behavior	This includes early involvement in any number of a variety of antisocial activities. Major indicators include being arrested at a young age, a large number of prior offenses, and rule violations while on conditional release.	History cannot be changed, but targets for change include developing new noncriminal behaviors in high-risk situations and building self-efficacy beliefs supportive of reform.
Antisocial Personality Pattern	People with this factor are impulsive, adventurous, pleasure-seeking, involved in generalized trouble, restlessly aggressive, and show a callous disregard for others.	Building skills to address weak self-control, anger management, and poorproblem-solving.
Antisocial Cognition	People with this factor hold attitudes, beliefs, values, rationalizations, and personal identity that is favorable to crime. Specific indicators include identifying with criminals, negative attitudes towards the law and justice system, beliefs that crime will yield rewards, and rationalizations that justify criminal behavior (e.g., the "victim deserved it").	Reducing antisocial thinking and feelings through building and practicing less risky thoughts and feelings.
Antisocial Associates	This factor includes both association with procriminal others and isolations from anticriminal others.	Reduce association with procriminal others and increase association with anticriminal others.

Risk/Need Factor	Indicator	Target for Intervention
	The Moderate Four	
Family/Marital Circumstances	Poor-quality relationships between either the child and the parent (in the case of juvenile offenders) or spouses (in the case of adult offenders) in combination with either neutral expectations with regards to crime or procriminal expectations.	Reduce conflict, build positive relationships, and enhance monitoring and supervision.
School/Work	Low levels of performance and involvement and low levels of rewards and satisfaction.	Enhance performance, involvement, rewards, and satisfaction.
Leisure/Recreation	Low levels of involvement in and satisfaction from noncriminal leisure pursuits.	Enhance involvement in and satisfaction from noncriminal leisure activities.
Substance Abuse	Problems with abusing alcohol and/or other drugs (excluding tobacco). Current problems with substance abuse indicate a higher risk than past substance abuse problems.	Reduce substance abuse, reduce the personal and interpersonal supports for substance-oriented behavior, and enhance alternatives to substance abuse.

Source: Adapted from Table 2.5 in D.A. Andrews and James Bonta, The Psychology of Criminal Conduct, 5th ed. (New Providence, NJ: Anderson Publishing, 2010).

Empirical Basis for the RNR Principles

Research on the risk principle suggests that recidivism is only reduced when high-risk offenders are placed in programs where they receive intensive levels of services.[40] In some instances, research also found that low-risk offenders who were placed in intensive treatment programs actually had an increased likelihood of recidivism.[41] This could be because placing low-risk offenders in intensive programming interrupts support structures or self-correcting behaviors that already exist, or because it exposes low-risk offenders to high-risk offenders who may have a negative influence on low-risk offenders' thoughts or behaviors.[42]

Research suggests that programs that adhere to the RNR principles are more effective at reducing recidivism.[43] Specifically, the more of the RNR principles a treatment program adheres to, the greater the reduction in recidivism. Research also indicates that treatment can be more effective when provided in a community setting, though treatment that adheres to the RNR principles can still be effective when provided in a custodial setting (i.e., prison or jail).

The developers of the RNR principles argue that research results indicate that the "central eight" risk and needs factors are the best predictors of future criminal behavior. A review of eight meta-analyses on the relationship between certain risk and needs factors and criminal behavior found moderate effect sizes for both the "big four" and the "moderate four" risk factors. In comparison, the mean effect size for four minor risk factors was not statistically significant.

CRITIQUES OF RISK AND NEEDS ASSESSMENT

Proponents assert that risk and needs assessment instruments are effective enough that they can help officials make decisions about who needs to be incarcerated and who can be safely treated and supervised in the community. However, while risk and needs assessment instruments have demonstrated the ability to predict the risk of recidivism with some degree of accuracy, there are people who are concerned about how these instruments are used in the criminal justice system. One expert notes that risk and needs assessment involves judgments about uncertainty.[44] Risk and needs assessment can limit the range of plausible speculation about a potential outcome, but it will never be certain. This expert notes that there are so many determinants of human behavior that it is impossible to reason through all of the possible outcomes. This section of the report provides an overview of some of the critiques of risk and needs assessment.

Making Judgments about Individuals Based on Group Tendencies

One of the key critiques of risk and needs assessment is that while there is evidence of some predictability in group behavior, it is difficult, if not impossible, to make a determination about how individual members of a group will behave.[45]

Two scholars argue that "[o]n the basis of empirical finding, statistical theory, and logic, we conclude that predictions of future offending [using risk and needs assessment] cannot be achieved in the individual case with any degree of confidence."[46] They note that it is a logical fallacy to make a causal inference about a member of a group based on the group's characteristics.[47]

However, the supposition that risk and needs assessment provides no useful information for criminal justice decision making has been vigorously contested. Two scholars assert that while the probabilities associated with assessment clearly will never be certain, group data can help criminal justice professionals make decisions about who is at risk of recidivating.[48] Proponents of the use of assessment note that the insurance industry makes decisions about risk based on actuarial methods.[49] Insurance companies set the price for insurance on a purchaser's membership in a group. Without relying on such probabilities it would be impossible for insurance companies to set prices.

However, researchers who question the use of risk and needs assessment to predict individual risk assert that this analogy is false because insurance companies are interested in predicting what proportion of insured individuals will, for example, die within a certain time frame; they are not interested in predicting the deaths of certain individuals.[50]

Should Risk Assessment Be Separate from Needs Assessment?

Research suggests that including dynamic risk factors in risk and needs assessment can increase its accuracy.[51] However, some experts in the field have also advocated for shorter risk assessment instruments that focus on a relatively short list of static risk factors.

One scholar of risk and needs assessment argues that risk and needs should not be measured together. He notes that many early assessment instruments were simple and consisted of fewer than a dozen factors.[52] More recently the focus of risk assessment has changed from solely predicting risk to "risk reduction." The focus on risk reduction means that instruments added dynamic risk factors that can change with time and/or are amenable to treatment and, therefore, reduce the offender's risk level.[53] However, some research has shown that *some* dynamic risk factors are not related to any measure of recidivism.[54] Also, dynamic risk factors might be more difficult to measure accurately.[55] It is argued that the inclusion of a bevy of dynamic risk factors has diluted the ability of risk and needs assessment instruments to classify cases accurately.[56] Most assessment instruments, even though they contain risk factors that might be extraneous to predicting risk, contain enough valid risk factors that they are able to predict with modest accuracy which groups of offenders are the most likely to recidivate. However, "[t]here is substantial evidence available to suggest that relatively brief risk indices outperform longer, more complex models."[57] For example, one study in Pennsylvania found that risk assessment accuracy was improved by using only 8 of the 54 factors in one commonly used instrument.

Two scholars have argued that risk assessment should be conducted separately from needs assessment.[58] Combining risk and needs assessment has the potential to introduce variables that might be useful when trying to assess what interventions would be effective to *reduce* an offender's risk, but it might reduce the ability of the instrument to predict risk accurately in situations where *only* predicting risk is all that is warranted (e.g., should someone be granted pretrial release or should an inmate be released on parole).

Potential for Discriminatory Effects

There is a concern that the wide-scale use of risk and needs assessment might exacerbate racial disparities in the nation's prison systems. One scholar contends that research on assessment instruments has not adequately vetted the tools for use on racial minorities.[59] This scholar notes that social context, such as gender, race, and economic and socio-structural factors, plays a role in crime, and assessment does not account for these factors.[60]

It is also possible that minorities might score higher on risk and needs assessments because "of their elevated exposure to risk, racial discrimination, and social inequality—not necessarily because of their criminal propensities or the crimes perpetrated."[61] One expert noted that most instruments use socioeconomic factors that correlate with race and ethnicity, and include factors that punish people for choices that people are allowed to make in a free society (e.g., whether to get married, live in a stable residence, or have a regular job).[62]

Another researcher has warned of the need to thoroughly evaluate risk and needs assessment instruments to ensure that the classifications of risk are not biased against African-Americans and Hispanics.[63] Cutoff points developed using reoffending rates for white offenders might lead to over- or under-classification for some minorities.

A review of the research on the relationship between race/ethnicity and predictive validity of risk and needs assessment found contradictory and mixed results.[64] The researchers found a total of eight meta-analyses that evaluated the role that race/ethnicity played in mediating the ability of instruments to predict recidivism. Three studies found that the higher the percentage of white offenders in the sample, the higher the predictive validity of the instrument—suggesting that instruments can better predict risk for white offenders. The other five studies found no evidence that predictive validity varied based on the race/ethnicity of the participants.

SELECT ISSUES FOR CONGRESS

There are four pieces of legislation before Congress that would establish a risk and needs assessment system in the BOP. The above discussion about the strengths and weaknesses of assessment might raise a question among some policymakers about whether the BOP should use a risk and needs assessment system. Even if policymakers decide that the BOP should use assessment, there might be additional questions about how to implement an effective assessment system. The four legislative proposals might also raise questions about whether other measures should be taken in order to reduce the number of inmates in federal prisons. This section of the report discusses some of the issues that might arise if Congress considers any of the current legislative proposals.

Should Risk and Needs Assessment Be Used in Federal Prisons?

An overarching issue policymakers might consider is whether the BOP should use risk and needs assessment. Research suggests that assessment instruments can make distinctions between high-and low-risk offenders with some degree of accuracy. Furthermore, assessment systems that adhere to the RNR principle appear to be effective at reducing recidivism. Implementing an assessment system in federal prisons would appear, based on the current research, to be an evidence-based way to improve the effectiveness of rehabilitative programming, and when combined with additional time credits for some inmates who participate in rehabilitative programs and productive activities, it might provide a means for reducing the federal prison population without increasing the risk to public safety.

However, risk and needs assessment systems are not flawless. There will always be false positives (e.g., inmates who are determined to be high risk but are actually a low risk for recidivism) even though the predictive accuracy of instruments has improved over the years with more research into the correlates of crime and the development of a theory of criminal behavior and effective rehabilitation (i.e., the RNR model).

There are also concerns that the use of risk and needs assessment will have a discriminatory effect on minorities. As discussed previously, the research on the applicability of currently used instruments for minorities is mixed. Some policymakers might be concerned that instruments might find minorities to be at a higher risk for recidivism than whites because of the use of static risk factors, such as criminal history, that might be more prevalent in minority communities because they are more at risk of coming into contact with the criminal justice system. While this is a valid concern, it should also be noted that many commonly used instruments consider a wide variety of dynamic risk factors that could allow all inmates to reduce their assessed risk level. Also, actuarial assessment is the norm, which makes the process of assessing each offender's risk level more objective. Before the use of actuarial assessment, decisions about who was to be assigned to which treatment program and who was to be released on parole were left to criminal justice professionals who made assessments based on their own sets of standards, which might have been influenced by overt or subconscious biases.

Should Certain Inmates Be Excluded from Earning Additional Time Credits?

One issue policymakers might consider is whether certain inmates should be excluded from earning extra time credits for participating in rehabilitative programs and productive activities. Some legislative proposals would exclude inmates who were convicted of certain offenses, such as violent and sex offenses, from earning additional time credits for participating in rehabilitative programming.[65] Research suggests that inmates should be assessed for risk and decisions about programming and supervision should be made based on those assessments regardless of the inmate's current offense. However, it might be argued that inmates who are convicted of serious offenses, such as violent or sex offenses, should not be eligible to be released from prison early, regardless of what they do to reduce their risk of recidivism.

Another issue that policymakers might consider is whether excluding inmates convicted for certain offenses would have a disparate effect on racial or ethnic minorities. Some policymakers might be concerned that excluding inmates convicted of certain offenses from being eligible to receive additional time credits under the proposed assessment system might mean that inmates of color would be more likely to have to serve more time in prison. However, this would only be true to the extent that inmates of color are more likely to be convicted of offenses that would make inmates ineligible to receive additional time credits. Data available through the Bureau of Justice Statistics' Federal Criminal Case Processing Statistics program is not detailed enough to allow CRS to analyze the potential disparate effects of the exclusions listed in the current legislative proposals. Congress might consider whether it wants to ask the U.S. Sentencing Commission or the BOP to assess the potential effects of excluding inmates convicted for certain offenses.

Should Priority Be Given to High-Risk Offenders?

Policymakers might consider whether the proposed risk and needs assessment system should focus on high-risk inmates. The RNR principles state that high-risk individuals should be the focus of interventional programming.

Research on the risk principle suggests that recidivism is only reduced when high-risk offenders are placed in programs where they receive intensive levels of services.[66] In some instances, research also found that low-risk offenders who were placed in intensive treatment programs actually had an increased likelihood of recidivism.[67] This could be because placing low-risk offenders in intensive programming interrupts support structures or self-correcting behaviors that already exist, or because it exposes low-risk offenders to high-risk offenders who may have a negative influence on low-risk offenders' thoughts or behaviors.[68] Some legislative proposals would require the BOP to phase-in the risk and needs assessment system.[69] During the phase-in period, low-risk prisoners would be given priority for programs and activities over moderate- and high-risk prisoners. In addition, higher-risk inmates would be required to participate in more rehabilitative programming, but inmates with low or no risk of recidivating would also be required to participate in rehabilitative programming. Other legislative proposals would require inmates who are deemed to be low risk and without need of recidivism reduction programming to continue to participate in productive activities.[70] Policymakers might consider whether inmates who are deemed to be low risk should immediately be placed in prerelease custody in order to open spots for moderate- and high-risk inmates who are in need of rehabilitative programming.

Should Risk and Needs Assessment Be Used in Sentencing?

Another issue policymakers might consider is whether risk and needs assessment should be used in sentencing to help identify low-risk offenders who could be diverted to community supervision rather than incarcerated. As discussed previously, research suggests that low-risk offenders should not be subjected to intensive treatment (and some research indicates that it might be criminogenic) and they might be able to be effectively supervised in the community. Some legislation would require the BOP, to the extent practicable, to house low-risk inmates together, which might help reduce the criminogenic effects of placing low-risk offenders in prison.[71] Legislative proposals would also seek ways to try to place some inmates in prerelease custody earlier.[72] However, if the purpose of the legislation is to reduce the federal prison population and save money, it is significantly cheaper to place offenders on probation compared to incarcerating them.[73]

While some scholars have argued for integrating risk assessment into sentencing guidelines to help judges determine the appropriate sentences for offenders,[74] research suggests that if such assessment were to be integrated into sentencing, it might be best to use it as a way to screen-out low-risk offenders. Three researchers who conducted a meta-analysis of the research on risk assessment instruments concluded that instruments could be used to make informed decisions about treatment or management of offenders.[75] However, the high number of false positives limits their effectiveness as a tool to make decisions about who should be sent to prison for longer periods of incarceration because they pose the greatest threat of reoffending. Simply stated, if assessment were to be used to make decisions about who should be incarcerated for long periods of time because certain offenders were at a high risk for committing more offenses, there is the potential to incarcerate a significant number of people who would not commit any more offenses. The researchers concluded that the results of their analysis "suggest that these tools can effectively screen out individuals at low risk of future offending."[76]

However, the idea of using risk and needs assessment in sentencing is not without controversy. DOJ, while acknowledging the important role the use of evidence-based practices plays in effective rehabilitation programs and reentry practices, has raised concerns about making risk assessment a part of determining sentences for federal offenders.[77] DOJ echoes previously mentioned concerns that risk assessment bases decisions on group dynamics and that determining someone's risk of reoffending on static risk factors might place certain groups of offenders at a disadvantage. DOJ also argues that using risk assessment in determining sentences would erode the certainty in sentencing, something Congress attempted to address when it passed the Sentencing Reform Act (P.L. 98-473), which eliminated parole for federal inmates and established a determinate sentencing structure under the federal sentencing guidelines. Certainty in sentencing, argues DOJ, is a key factor in deterring crime. DOJ also argues that sentencing should primarily be about holding offenders accountable for past criminal behavior.

Should There Be a Decreased Emphasis on Punishment?

If Congress were to consider legislation to implement risk and needs assessment in the federal prison system, policymakers might consider whether implementing a policy of making decisions based on an offender's risk level is compatible with a perceived desire to continue to incarcerate certain offenders for as long as possible. Some legislation would exempt inmates convicted of certain crimes from being eligible from earning extra time credits.[78] This would mean that offenders convicted of certain offenses would be required to serve a greater proportion of their sentences in prison even if they are deemed to be at a low risk for recidivism. As discussed previously, it is an offender's past history of antisocial behavior, and not the offender's current offense, that is indicative of a risk for recidivism. Therefore, the policy of requiring certain offenders to serve most of their sentences in prison might, in some capacity, undermine the potential effectiveness of a risk and needs assessment system.

Research has questioned the effectiveness of incarceration as a way to reduce crime. It suggests that while incarceration did contribute to lower violent crime rates in the 1990s, there are declining marginal returns associated with ever-increasing levels of incarceration.[79] The diminishing level of return resulting from higher levels of incarceration might be explained by the fact that higher levels of incarceration are likely to include more offenders who are either at the end of their criminal careers or who were at a low risk of committing crimes at a high rate (so-called "career criminals").[80] Another possible reason for diminishing marginal returns might be that more of the individuals incarcerated over the past three decades have been incarcerated for crimes where there is a high level of replacement (i.e., incarcerating one offender "opens the market" for a new offender to take that person's place).[81] For example, if a drug dealer is incarcerated and there is no decrease in demand for drugs in the drug market, it is possible that someone will step in to take that person's role; therefore, no further crimes may be averted by incarcerating the individual. It is also possible that being imprisoned with other offenders is actually criminogenic, especially for low-risk offenders.[82]

Research on the psychology of punishment also provides insight into why incarceration might provide a limited deterrent effect. For punishment to be successful at suppressing behavior it requires

- the immediate delivery of an intense level of punishment, □ catching and punishing criminals for every offense,
- not allowing the offender to be able to escape from the consequences of the behavior,
- making the density of the punishment associated with the behavior greater than the density of the rewards, and
- the punishment be consistent with the characteristics of the offender.[83]

However, "the necessary conditions for effective punishment are virtually impossible to meet for the criminal justice system. Police cannot be everywhere to ensure the certainty of detection, the courts cannot pass sentence quickly enough, and correctional officials have difficulties ensuring adequate supervision and monitoring."[84] There is also an argument to be made about the purpose of incarceration. While there might be a minimal general deterrent effect associated with incarceration, it does provide for incapacitation, which can reduce the number of crimes an incarcerated offender can commit. Also, long prison terms might provide for society's sense of justice. Sentencing someone to prison for several years, or even decades, could be viewed as a way for society to say that there are certain behaviors that will not be tolerated, and those who commit such transgressions deserve to receive severe punishment for them.

APPENDIX A. COMPARISON OF RISK AND NEEDS ASSESSMENT LEGISLATION

This appendix provides a comparison of the risk and needs assessment-related provisions in four bills introduced in the 114th Congress:

- S. 467, the CORRECTIONS Act;
- S. 2123, the Sentencing Reform and Corrections Act of 2015;
- H.R. 759, the Recidivism Risk Reduction Act; and
- H.R. 2944, the Sensenbrenner-Scott SAFE Justice Reinvestment Act of 2015.

The text of S. 2123 generally incorporates the text of S. 467, with a few key differences, highlighted below.

Establishment of an Assessment System

S. 467 and S. 2123 would require the Department of Justice (DOJ) to establish, within 30 months of the enactment of the bill, a Post-Sentencing Risk and Needs Assessment System (Assessment System) for use in the BOP that would

- assess and determine the recidivism risk level of all inmates and classify each inmate as being at low, moderate, or high risk for recidivism;
- to the extent practicable, determine the risk of violence for all inmates;
- ensure that, to the extent practicable, low-risk inmates are housed and assigned to programs together;
- assign inmates to rehabilitative programs and productive activities based on their risk level and criminogenic needs;
- periodically reassess and update an inmate's risk level and programmatic needs; and
- provide information on best practices concerning the tailoring of rehabilitative programs to the criminogenic needs of each inmate.

H.R. 759 would also require DOJ to develop and release an Assessment System for use by the BOP, but it would require DOJ to establish the system within 180 days of the bill becoming law. The requirements for the Assessment System under H.R. 759 are similar to those of S. 467, but H.R. 759 would *not* require the Assessment System to determine the risk of violence for all inmates, nor require that low-risk inmates be housed together and assigned to the same programs.

H.R. 2944 would require DOJ to develop an Assessment System within one year of the bill becoming law. The requirements for the system that would be established under H.R. 2944 are similar to those of the other two bills in that H.R. 2944 would require the system to be used to assess and determine the risk and needs factors for federal inmates and to assign inmates to recidivism reduction programs based on their risk and needs. The Assessment System that would be established by the bill would not be required to assess each inmate's risk of violence nor require low-risk inmates to be segregated. However, the bill notes that "some activities or excessive programming may be counter-productive for some prisoners" and as such, it would allow DOJ to provide guidance to the BOP on the quality and quantity of rehabilitative programming that is both appropriate and effective. All four pieces of legislation would require DOJ, when developing the Assessment System, to use the best available research and best practices in the field of risk and needs assessment. S. 467, S. 2123, and H.R. 759 would allow DOJ to develop its own instrument or use an existing instrument. H.R. 2944 would require DOJ to prescribe a "suitable intake assessment tool" but it is silent as to whether the instrument would need to be developed in-house or if an existing instrument could be used. In addition, all four bills would require DOJ either to validate the instrument on the federal prison population or to ensure that the instrument has been validated using federal inmates.

S. 2123 would also require DOJ to make adjustments to the system on a regular basis, but not less than once every three years. In doing so, DOJ would be required to consider the best evidence available on effective means of reducing recidivism rates and to make adjustments, to the extent possible, to ensure that the system does not result in any unwarranted disparities, including disparities amongst similarly classified inmates of different racial groups. S. 2123 would require DOJ to adjust the system to reduce disparities to the greatest extent possible. The bill would also require DOJ to coordinate with the U.S. Probation and Pretrial Services Office to ensure that the findings of each offender's presentence report are available and considered in the Assessment System.

Expanding Rehabilitative Programs

S. 467 and S. 2123 would require the BOP, subject to the availability of appropriations, to make recidivism reduction programs and productive activities available to all eligible inmates within six years of enactment of the legislation. Both bills would also require the National Institute of Corrections to evaluate all programs and activities to ensure that they are evidence based and effective at reducing recidivism.

H.R. 2944 would require the BOP, subject to the availability of appropriations, to make recidivism reduction programs and productive activities available to all eligible inmates within one year of enactment.

H.R. 759 would also require the BOP to expand, subject to appropriations, recidivism reduction programs and productive activities for inmates. However, H.R. 759 would phase in expansion of programs and activities. The BOP would be required to provide rehabilitative programming and productive programs to 20% of inmates within one year of the date when risk and needs assessments are completed for all inmates. The BOP would be required to provide rehabilitative programming and productive activities to an additional 20% of inmates each year until they are serving all inmates. During the phase-in period, low-risk inmates would be given first priority for participation in rehabilitative programs and productive activities. Moderate- and high-risk inmates would be given second and third priority, respectively. Also, within risk levels, priority would be given to inmates who are closer to finishing their sentences. All four bills would allow the BOP to enter into partnerships with nonprofit organizations, educational institutions, and private entities in order to provide rehabilitative programs and activities for inmates. S. 2123 would also allow the BOP to enter into partnerships with "industry-sponsored organizations that deliver workforce development and training that lead to recognized certification and employment."

Assessing the Risk and Needs of Inmates

S. 467 and S. 2123 would require the BOP to conduct an initial risk and needs assessment for all inmates within 30 months of the bill becoming law. Both bills would also require the BOP to reassess each inmate at least once a year for inmates within three years of release; at least once every other year for inmates who are within 10 years of release; and at least once every three years for every other inmate.

H.R. 759 would require the BOP to periodically reassess inmates who successfully participate in rehabilitative programs and productive activities (with high- and moderate-risk inmates receiving more frequent evaluations) and assign inmates to the proper programs and activities if their risk levels change.

H.R. 2944 would require the BOP to develop a case plan for each inmate that targets each inmate's risk and needs and helps guide the inmate's rehabilitation. Case plans would have to be completed within 30 days of an inmate's initial admission. Case plans would be required to

- include programming and treatment requirements based on the inmate's assessed risk and needs;
- ensure that inmates whose risk and needs do not warrant recidivism reduction programming participate in and successfully complete productive activities, including prison jobs; and
- ensure that eligible inmates participate in and successfully complete recidivism reduction programming or productive activities throughout their entire term of incarceration.

H.R. 2944 would require the BOP to provide each inmate with a copy of the case plan and discuss the case plan with the inmate. The BOP would be required to review the case plan with the inmate every six month to assess the inmate's progress towards completing it and whether the inmate needs to participate in additional or different rehabilitative programs.

Training for Staff on Using the Assessment System

All four bills would require BOP staff who are responsible for administering the Assessment System to be trained on how to properly use the system, which includes a requirement that staff demonstrate competence in administering the instrument. S. 467, S. 2123, and H.R. 759 would require DOJ to monitor and assess the use of the Assessment System and to periodically audit the use of the system in BOP facilities. H.R. 2944 would require DOJ, the Government Accountability Office, and DOJ's Inspector General's Office to monitor and assess the use of the Assessment System and to conduct separate and independent periodic audits of the use of the system.

Additional Time Credits and Other Incentives

S. 467 and S. 2123 would grant additional time credit for inmates who successfully complete 30 days of rehabilitative programming and productive activities. Every inmate would be eligible to earn five additional days of credit upon completion. Inmates who are deemed low risk would be eligible to receive an additional five days. S. 467 would exempt the following inmates from earning additional time credits:

- inmates serving a sentence for a second federal offense;
- inmates who were in the highest criminal history category under the U.S. Sentencing Guidelines at the time of sentencing; and
- any inmate sentenced for a terrorism offense,85 a crime of violence,86 a sex offense,[87] racketeering,[88] engaging in a continuing corrupt criminal enterprise,[89] a federal fraud offense for which the inmate was sentenced to more than 15 years' imprisonment, or a crime involving child exploitation.[90]

S. 2123 would exempt the following inmates from earning additional time credits:

- inmates serving a sentence for a second federal offense, which would not include any offense under the Major Crimes Act (relating to federal jurisdiction over certain enumerated crimes committed by Native Americans on tribal lands) for which the offender was sentenced to less than 13 months;
- inmates who have 13 or more criminal history points, as determined under the U.S. Sentencing Guidelines, at the time of sentencing, unless the court determines in writing that the defendant's criminal history score substantially over-represents the seriousness of the offender's criminal history or the likelihood that the offender will commit other crimes;
- any inmate sentenced for a terrorism offense,[91] a crime of violence,[92] a sex offense,[93] engaging in a continuing corrupt criminal enterprise,[94] or a federal fraud offense for which the inmate was sentenced to more than 15 years' imprisonment, a crime involving child exploitation;[95] or

- inmates convicted of offenses under chapter 11 (relating to bribery, graft, and conflicts of interest); chapter 29 (relating to elections and political activities); chapter 63 (involving a scheme or artifice to deprive someone of the intangible right of honest services); chapter 73 (relating to the obstruction of justice); chapter 95 or 96 (relating to racketeering and racketeering influenced and corrupt organizations); chapter 110 (relating sexual abuse and other abuse of children); or sections 1028A, 1031, or 1040 (relating to fraud) of Title 18 of the U.S. Code.

H.R. 759 would also allow inmates to earn additional time credits for successfully participating in rehabilitative programs or productive activities, but the credit structure would be different. Under H.R. 759, low-risk inmates would be eligible to receive 30 days of time credits for each month they successfully participate in a rehabilitative program or productive activity; moderate-risk inmates would be eligible to receive 15 days, and high-risk inmates would be eligible to receive 8 days. H.R. 759 lists 47 offenses that would make federal inmates ineligible to receive additional time credits for participating in rehabilitative programs or productive activities. The enumerated offenses could generally be classified as violent offenses, terrorism offenses, espionage offenses, human trafficking offenses, sex and sexual exploitation offenses, and high-level drug offenses.[96] The bill would also exclude inmates with three or more convictions for crimes of violence or drug trafficking offenses.

H.R. 2944 would allow inmates to earn 10 days of time credits for each month they successfully comply with their case plans. Unlike the other two pieces of legislation, under H.R. 2944 all inmates would be eligible to receive the same amount of time credits, regardless of risk score. Also, unlike the two other pieces of legislation, H.R. 2944 would allow the BOP to retroactively award time credits to eligible inmates for participating in rehabilitative programs and activities before enactment of the bill. Inmates who have been convicted of murder,[97] terrorism,[98] or sex offenses[99] would not be eligible to receive time credits for participating in rehabilitative programming.

S. 467, S. 2123, and H.R. 2944 would require the BOP to develop other incentives, such as additional telephone or visitation privileges, for inmates who are exempt from earning additional time credits. H.R. 759 would allow any prisoner who successfully participates in a rehabilitative program or productive activity to receive, for use with family, close friends, mentors, and religious leaders, up to 30 minutes per day and up to 900 minutes per month in phone privileges and, as determined by the facility's warden, additional visitation time.

H.R. 2944 would require the BOP to amend its inmate disciplinary program to provide for the reduction of earned time credits for inmates who violate institutional rules or the rules of the rehabilitative program or productive activity.[100] The amendments would be required to specify the level of violations and the corresponding penalties; that any loss of earned time credits does not apply to earning credits in the future; and a procedure for inmates to have lost time credits restored based on their progress. H.R. 759 includes a similar requirement. S. 467 and S. 2123 would allow the BOP to reduce earned time credits for misbehavior, but it would not require the BOP to do so.

Under both S. 467 and S. 2123, inmates would not be allowed to accrue the proposed additional time credits if the inmate has accrued other time credits for participation in another program under another provision of law. Under both House bills, the time credits earned for participating in rehabilitative programs and productive activities would be in addition to any other rewards or incentives for which inmates might be eligible.

Placement in Prerelease Custody

The extra time credit inmates could earn under S. 467, S. 2123, and H.R. 759 would allow them to be placed on prerelease custody earlier. Under both S. 467 and S. 2123, inmates who are deemed to be at a low risk for recidivism within one year of being eligible to be placed in prerelease custody, or inmates who are deemed at a moderate risk for recidivism but their most recent risk and needs assessment shows that their risk of recidivism has decreased, would be eligible to be placed in a residential reentry center (RRC, i.e., a halfway house) or home confinement. Inmates who are deemed to be low risk for recidivism can be placed on community supervision. Inmates who have earned less than 36 months of additional good time credit would only be eligible to spend one-half of that time on community supervision, while inmates who have earned 36 months or more of additional good time credit would be eligible to serve the amount of such credit exceeding 18 months on community supervision.

H.R. 759 would allow the BOP to place inmates who are deemed to be low risk, who have earned time credits equal to the amount of time remaining on their sentences, and who are otherwise deemed qualified, in prerelease custody. All inmates transferred to prerelease custody would be placed on home confinement. Inmates would be required to remain on home confinement until they served at least 85% of their imposed sentence.

Under both Senate bills, any period of supervised release imposed on an inmate would be reduced by the amount of time the prisoner spent in prerelease custody. Inmates would not be eligible to be transferred to community supervision unless the amount of time the inmate could spend on community supervision is equal to or greater than the amount of time remaining on the inmate's period of prerelease custody.

H.R. 2944 does not contain any provisions related to special conditions for inmates placed on prerelease custody pending completion of their sentences.

Judicial Review of Prerelease Custody Placement

Both S. 467 and S. 2123 would not allow the BOP to transfer any inmate sentenced to more than three years of incarceration to prerelease custody unless the BOP provides notice to the U.S. Attorney's office in the district where the inmate was convicted. The federal government would be allowed to challenge an inmate's prerelease custody. A court would be allowed to deny an inmate's transfer to prerelease custody or modify the terms of such transfer if, after conducting a hearing, the court finds by a preponderance of the evidence that placing the inmate on prerelease custody is inconsistent with the factors specified in paragraphs (2), (6), and (7) of 18 U.S.C. §3553(a).

H.R. 759 would require the BOP to notify the court in the district in which the inmate was convicted of its intention to place the inmate in prerelease custody. A judge would be required to approve or deny the recommendation within 30 days. However, the judge would only be able to deny the recommendation if he or she finds through clear and convincing evidence that the inmate's actions after conviction warrant denial of the transfer to prerelease custody. Failure of the judge to approve or deny the recommendation within 30 days would be treated as an approval.

None of the bills contain language that would allow inmates to appeal a court's decision to deny them placement in prerelease custody.

Judicial Review of Prerelease Custody Placement

Both S. 467 and S. 2123 would not allow the BOP to transfer any inmate sentenced to more than three years of incarceration to prerelease custody unless the BOP provides notice to the U.S. Attorney's office in the district where the inmate was convicted. The federal government would be allowed to challenge an inmate's prerelease custody. A court would be allowed to deny an inmate's transfer to prerelease custody or modify the terms of such transfer if, after conducting a hearing, the court finds by a preponderance of the evidence that placing the inmate on prerelease custody is inconsistent with the factors specified in paragraphs (2), (6), and (7) of 18 U.S.C. §3553(a).

H.R. 759 would require the BOP to notify the court in the district in which the inmate was convicted of its intention to place the inmate in prerelease custody. A judge would be required to approve or deny the recommendation within 30 days. However, the judge would only be able to deny the recommendation if he or she finds through clear and convincing evidence that the inmate's actions after conviction warrant denial of the transfer to prerelease custody. Failure of the judge to approve or deny the recommendation within 30 days would be treated as an approval. None of the bills contain language that would allow inmates to appeal a court's decision to deny them placement in prerelease custody.

Appendix B. Commonly Used Risk and Needs Assessment Instruments

There are many different risk and/or needs assessment instruments currently available. Some are only comprised of static risk factors while some use a combination of static and dynamic risk factors. Some are used to predict general recidivism while others focus on predicting recidivism for certain populations of offenders, such as sex offenders or domestic abusers. *Table B-1* presents a summary of the key aspects of seven commonly used risk and needs assessment instruments. The information provided in *Table B-1* is meant to provide examples of the differences in how some risk and needs assessment instruments are developed, the requirements to administer them, and the items they use to assess risk and needs.

Table B-1. Commonly Used Risk and Needs Assessment Instruments

Instrument	Background Information	Administration Requirements	Instrument Contents
Correctional Offender Management Profiling for Alternative Sanctions (COMPAS)	The original COMPAS system was created in the late 1990s. The instrumentwas designed to assess key risk and needs factors in adult and youth correctional populations and to provide decision support for practitioners charged with case planning and management. COMPAS can assess four types of risk (general recidivism, violent recidivism, non-compliance, and failure to appear). Originally developed and validated usingoffenders in New York, COMPAS has since been modifiedas revalidation data offersnew insights on the performance and validity of the instrument.	COMPAS allows for some degree of flexibility in the administration process. Offender data collection options include offender self-report, scripted interviews, and structured interviews as part of a web-based, automated assessment process. The developeroffers training that covers practical use, interpretation of results, and case planning strategies. Advanced training options are available on the theoretical underpinnings of offender assessments, gender responsivity training, motivational interviewing, and other topics.	The COMPAS Core assessment for adult offenders contains both static and dynamic factors. Content may be individually tailored based on jurisdictional needs and resources, but can include four risk and four need scales: • Risk: failure to appear, non-compliance (technical violations), general recidivism, violent recidivism. • Criminogenic needs: cognitive-behavioral, criminal associates/peers criminal involvement, criminal opportunity, criminal personality, criminal thinking (self-report), current violence, family criminality, financial problems, history of non-compliance, history of violence, leisure/boredom, residential instability, social adjustment,

Instrument	Background Information	Administration Requirements	Instrument Contents
			social environment, social isolation, socialization failure, substance abuse, vocation/education
Inventory of Offender Risk, Needs, and Strengths (IORNS)	IORNS was created in 2006 as an offender assessment of static risk, dynamic risk/need, and protective strength factors. The tool is complemented by several subscales for specific assessments in the areas of violent and sexual criminal behavior.	Administratorsmust hold a degree in forensic or clinical psychology or psychiatry plus satisfactory completion of appropriate coursework in psychological testing, or have a license or certification from an agency that requires such training and experience. Line staff can administer the self-report assessment to offenders and score the results, but they must be supervised by a licensed professional who is also responsible for interpreting the instrument.	IORNS is a 130-item true/false self-report questionnaire that assesses static risk, dynamic risk/need, and protective strength factors in separate indices. It consists of four total indices and eight scales. • The Static Risk Index (SRI) contains12 criminal history items. • The Dynamic Need Index (DNI) contains 79 items in the form of six dynamic need scales: Criminal Orientation, Psychopathy, Intra/Interpersonal Problems, Alcohol/Drug Problems, • Aggression, and Negative Social Influences. The Protective Strength Index (PSI) contains 26 items in the form of two scales: Personal Resources and Environmental Resources.

Table B-1. (Continued)

Instrument	Background Information	Administration Requirements	Instrument Contents
Level of Service Inventory-Revised (LSI-R), Level of Service/Case Management Inventory (LS/CMI), and Level of Service/Risk, Need, Responsivity (LS/RNR)	LSI-R was developed in 1995 and validated using a Canadian criminal population. It is a "third generation" risk and needs assessment instrument. LS/CMI is the "fourth generation" revision of LSI-R that assesses offender risk, needs, and responsivity (RNR) to inform caseplanning via a built-in case management system. The LS/RNR is similarly comprised of the updated risk, need, and responsivity scales, but offer these separately from the LS/CMI case management system for organizations already equipped with established case management systems of their own.	LSI-R and LS/CMI are administered through a structured interview between the interviewer and offender, with the recommendation that supporting documentation be collected from family members, employers, case files, drug tests, and other relevant sources as needed. Those who administer the exam must have an understanding of the principles of tests and measurements or be supervised by someone who does; a professional with advanced training in psychological assessment or a related discipline must assume responsibility for the instrument's use, interpretation, and communication of results.	LSI-R and LS/CMI contain a mix of static and dynamic factors, developed from recidivism literature, professional opinions of probation officers, and relevant social learning theory on criminal behavior. LSI-R is a 54-item risk and needs assessment instrument that consists of 10 areas: Criminal History, Education and Employment, Financial, Family and Marital, Accommodations, Leisure and Recreation, Companions, Alcohol/Drug Problems, Emotional/Personal, and Attitudes/Orientation. LS/CMI refined and combined content ofthe LSI-R into 43 items in 8 sections: Criminal History, Education/Employment, Family/Marital, Leisure/Recreation, Companions, Alcohol/Drug Problems, Procriminal Attitude/Orientation, and Antisocial Pattern.

Instrument	Background Information	Administration Requirements	Instrument Contents
			LS/CMI system contains seven additional sections. Sections 2-5 of LS/CMI identify additional risk factors (personal problems; social, health, and responsivityconsiderations; perpetration history; mental health; procriminal attitude /orientation; incarceration history, and concerns). Sections 6-7 provide a summary of risks and needs, allowing for clinical overrides of assessment recommendations based on atypical offender situations. Section 8 provides tools for program and placement decisions.
Ohio Risk Assessment System (ORAS)	ORAS was developed in 2006 as a collaborative effort between the Ohio Department of Rehabilitation & Correction (DRC) andthe University of Cincinnati Center for Criminal Justice Research (CCJR).	No specialized education is necessary to administer ORAS. However, researchers at CCJR have assembled a mandatory training package for those interested in using ORAS.	ORAS consists of 101 items divided between six tools. All tools contain bothstatic and dynamic factors. The tools in ORAS are • PretrialAssessment Tool; • Community Supervision Screening Tool;

Table B-1. (Continued)

Instrument	Background Information	Administration Requirements	Instrument Contents
	The goal was to create a consistent, reliable, standardized system of tools that could be used at various decision points in the criminal justice system to facilitate communication and continuity across criminal justice agencies. ORAS is a"fourth generation"assessment instrument.	ORAS uses a combination of structured interviews, official records, and other collateral sources tocomplete the assessment instrument. Offenders also completea self-report questionnaire to supplement this information.	• Community Supervision Tool: assesses criminal history, education,employment, and financial situation, family and social support, neighborhood problems, substance use, peer associations, and criminal attitudes and behavioral patterns; • Prison Screening Tool; • Prison Intake Tool (PIT): assesses age, criminal history, school behavior and employment, family and social support, substance abuse and mental health, and criminal lifestyle; and • Prison Reentry Tool: assesses age, criminal history, social bonds, and criminal attitudes and behavioral patterns.

Instrument	Background Information	Administration Requirements	Instrument Contents
Offender Screening Tool (OST)	In 1998, the Maricopa County (Arizona) Adult Probation Department (MCAPD), working with consultant Dr. David Simourd, developed and implemented its own assessment instrument, the Offender Screening Tool (OST).MCAPD originally sought to createa risk/needs tool that would (1) provide a broad, overall assessment of offender risk/needs, (2) incorporate static and dynamic risk factors most predictive of criminal behavior, (3) provide information that could be used to determine risk of recidivism and guide case planning/management decisions, and (4) be meaningful and valuable to staff.	OST is administered at the presentencing stage by interviewers who enter information into a computerized system for automated scoring. No specialized certifications are required, but all staff members receive training. In Maricopa County, the presentence division receives training on how to administer and interpret results from OST; all other probation department staff receive training on interpretation and how to use results to inform case planning and management.	The OST contains 44 items (14 static, 30dynamic) in 10 domains: • Vocational/Financial, • Education, • Family and Social Relationships, • Residence and Neighborhood, • Alcohol, • Drug Abuse, • Mental Health, • Attitude, and • Criminal Behavior. The final domain, Physical Health/Medical, is used exclusively as a responsivity factor.

Table B-1. (Continued)

Instrument	Background Information	Administration Requirements	Instrument Contents
	As a greater variety of cognitive-behavioral treatment programs became available in the county, Dr. Simourd and MCAPD expanded OST to include additional needs domains.OST was implemented statewide in 2005.		
Static Risk and Offender Needs Guide (STRONG)	In 1999, the Washington Legislature directedthe Department of Corrections (DOC) to improve the classification of felony offenders and to deploy staff and rehabilitative resources more effectively.	The Static Risk Assessment is conducted based on a thorough investigation of offender criminal history information. No offender interview is necessary. No specialized administrator qualifications are required to administer the Offender Needs Assessment; staff membersmay conduct the structured interview.	STRONG consists of two separate assessments. The Static Risk Assessmentis conducted first based on the offender's criminal history information and contains 26 items in the following domains: demographics, juvenile record, commitment to the DOC, total adult felony record, total adult misdemeanor record, and total sentence/upervision violations.

Instrument	Background Information	Administration Requirements	Instrument Contents
	The Washington State Institute for Public Policy (WSIPP) examined the validity of the risk instrument the DOC was using at the time (LSI-R) and thought that the predictive power of the assessment could be improved by including more static risk items. WSIPP, at the behest of DOC, createda newstatic risk instrument (Static Risk Assessment) comprised of only offender demographic and criminal history information, which was completed in 2006. In 2008, DOC implemented their automated offender assessment and case planning system.	It is recommended that line staff complete routine booster training sessions in addition to an initial training program for quality assurance purposes. For improved quality control, Washington established a small, dedicated intake unit to conduct all risk assessments statewide.	Calculated separately, the Offender Needs Assessment contains 55 items in 10 domains: education, community employment, friends, residential, family, alcohol/drug use, mental health, aggression, attitudes/behaviors, and

Table B-1. (Continued)

Instrument	Background Information	Administration Requirements	Instrument Contents
	This automated system included the Static Risk Assessment and an Offender Needs Assessment, which is used to identify offender needs and protective factors for use in case planning. STRONG is considered a "fourth generation" risk and needs assessment instrument.		
Wisconsin Risk/Needs Scales (WRN) and Correctional Assessment and Intervention System (CAIS)	The Wisconsin Classification System was created in 1977. This system is comprised of the Wisconsin Risk/Needs scales (WRN) and the Client Management Classification (CMC) responsivity and case management tool.	No specialized education is required; trained line staff can administer WRN or CAIS. NCCD developed and administersa training package for the CAIS tool.	WRN is a 53-item interview-driven assessment. Content areas include criminal history, education/ employment, family/friends, mental/emotional stability, plans/problems, health, sexual behavior, drug/alcohol usage, and financial management. The CMC is a 71-item interview-based case planning process that categorizes offenders into one of four possible typologies (Selective Intervention, Casework/Control, Environmental Structure, and Limit Setting).

Instrument	Background Information	Administration Requirements	Instrument Contents
	To facilitate practitioner use of the system, the National Council on Crime and Delinquency (NCCD) updated the tools in 2004 and created the automated, web-based Correctional Assessment and Intervention System (CAIS).		These classifications can then beused to guide case planning strategies. CAIS is an automated assessment and case management system that includes an updated version of WRN and CMC. A new risk and needs tool was created based on the results of a meta-analysis and can be includedin CAIS.

Source: CRS presentation of information provided in Appendix A to Pamela M Casey, Roger K. Warren, and Jennifer K. Elek, Using Offender Risk and Needs Assessment Information at Sentencing: Guidance for Courts from a National Working Group, National Center for State Courts, Williamsburg, VA, 2011.

End Notes

[1] University at Albany, School of Criminal Justice, Hindelang Criminal Justice Research Center, Sourcebook of Criminal Justice Statistics (online), Table 6.28.2012.

[2] E. Ann Carson, Prisoners in 2013, U.S. Department of Justice, Office of Justice Programs, Bureau of Justice Statistics, NCJ 247282, Washington, DC, September 2014, p. 2.

[3] Research by the Brennan Center for Justice and the New York University School of Law estimates that 0%-7% of the decline in crime in the 1990s can be attributed to increased incarceration, while 0%-1% of the decrease in crime since 2000 can be attributed to increased incarceration. Oliver Roeder, Lauren-Brooke Eisen, and Julia Bowling, What Caused the Crime Decline?, Brennan Center for Justice, New York, NY, February 12, 2015, p. 6.

[4] Anne Morrison Piehl and Bert Useem, "Prisons," in Crime and Public Policy, ed. Joan Petersilia and James Q. Wilson, 2nd ed. (New York: Oxford University Press, 2011), p. 542.

[5] See P.L. 113-76 and the joint explanatory statement to accompany P.L. 113-76, printed in the January 15, 2014, Congressional Record, p. H514.

[6] Leon Neyfakh, "OK, So Who Gets to Go Free?," Slate, March 4, 2015, http://www.slate.com/articles/ news_and_politics/crime/2015/03/prison_reform_releasing_only_nonviolent_offenders_won_t_get_you_very_far.html.

[7] Ibid.

[8] Eileen Sullivan and Ronnie Green, "States Predict Inmates' Future Crimes with Secretive Surveys," Associated Press, February 24, 2015, http://bigstory.ap.org/article/027a00d70782476eb7cd07fbcca40fc2/states-predict-inmates-futurecrimes-secretive-surveys.

[9] Edward J. Latessa and Brian Lovins, "The Role of Offender Risk Assessment: a Policy Maker Guide," Victims and Offenders, vol. 5, 2010, p. 212 (hereinafter "The Role of Offender Risk Assessment").

[10] See for example, S. 467, S. 2123, H.R. 759, and H.R. 2944. A more detailed comparison of the four bills can be found in Appendix A.

[11] Pew Center on the States, Risk/Needs Assessment 101: Science Reveals New Tools to Manage Offenders, issue brief, September 2011, http://www.pewtrusts.org/~/ media/ legacy/uploadedfiles/pcs_assets/2011/ PewRiskAssessmentbriefpdf.pdf, p. 2 (hereinafter, "Risk/Needs Assessment 101")

[12] Ibid.

[13] Ibid.

[14] James Austin, "The Proper and Improper Use of Risk Assessment in Corrections," Federal Sentencing Reporter, vol. 16, no. 3, February 2004, p. 5 (hereinafter "The Proper and Improper Use of Risk Assessment in Corrections")

[15] "Criminogenic" is commonly understood to mean factors that can contribute to criminal behavior.

[16] "The Proper and Improper Use of Risk Assessment in Corrections," p. 5.

[17] Appendix B provides information on some commonly used risk and needs assessment instruments.

[18] Public Safety Canada, Predicting Violent Recidivism, Research Summary, vol. 12, no. 3, May 2007, http://www.publicsafety.gc.ca/cnt/rsrcs/pblctns/prdtng-rcvds/index-eng.aspx; Mary Ann Campbell, Sheila French, and Paul Gendreau, "The Prediction of Violence in Adult Offenders; A Meta-Analytic Comparison of Instruments and Methods of Assessment," Criminal Justice and Behavior, vol. 36, no. 6, June 2009, pp. 567-590; Min Yang, Stephen

C.P. Wong, and Jeremy Coid, "The Efficacy of Violence Prediction: A Meta-Analytic Comparison of Nine Risk Assessment Tools," Psychological Bulletin, vol. 136, no. 5, 2010, pp. 740-767.

[19] Min Yang, Stephen C.P. Wong, and Jeremy Coid, "The Efficacy of Violence Prediction: A Meta-Analytic Comparison of Nine Risk Assessment Tools," Psychological Bulletin, vol. 136, no. 5, 2010, p. 757.

[20] Daryl G. Kroner, Jeremy F. Mills, and John R. Reddon, "A Coffee Can, Factor Analysis, and Prediction of Antisocial Behavior: The Structure of Criminal Risk," International Journal of Law and Psychology, vol. 28, 2005, pp. 360-374.

[21] John Monahan and Jennifer L. Skeem, "Risk Redux: The Resurgence of Risk Assessment in Criminal Sanctioning," Federal Sentencing Reporter, vol. 26, no. 3, February 2014, p. 162 (hereinafter "Risk Redux").

[22] Ibid.

[23] Vera Institute of Justice's Center of Sentencing and Corrections, Risk and Needs Assessment, memorandum to the Delaware Justice Reinvestment Task Force, October 12, 2011, pp. 9-12, https://ltgov.delaware.gov/taskforces/djrtf/ DJRTF_Risk_Assessment_Memo.pdf (hereinafter "Vera Institute of Justice's memorandum re: risk and needs assessment").

[24] The Role of Offender Risk Assessment, p. 205.

[25] Ibid.

[26] Ohio Department of Rehabilitation and Corrections, Ohio Risk Assessment System, http://www.drc.ohio.gov/web/ oras.htm.

[27] Edward J. Latessa, Richard Lemke, and Matthew Makarios, et al., "The Creation and Validation of the Ohio Risk Assessment System (ORAS)," Federal Probation, vol. 74, no. 1 (June 2010).

[28] Pamela M Casey, Roger K. Warren, and Jennifer K. Elek, Using Offender Risk and Needs Assessment Information at Sentencing: Guidance for Courts from a National Working Group, National Center for State Courts, Williamsburg, VA, 2011, p. 5.

[29] There are several principles other than risk, needs, and responsivity that are a part of the RNR model. These include three overarching principles: delivering services with respect for people, basing programs on psychological theory, and reducing criminal victimization. In addition to the risk, needs, and responsivity principles, there are several other core principles, including introducing human services in order to reduce recidivism, targeting more criminogenic needs relative to noncriminogenic needs, assessing offenders' strengths to enhance prediction and specific responsivity effects, using structured assessments, and only using professional discretion for very specific reasons. There are also three organizational principles: a preference for community-based services, services are enhanced when delivered by therapists and staff with high-quality relationships skills in combination with high-quality structuring skills, and management should closely oversee the provision of services. For a more detailed overview of all of the principles of the RNR model, see Chapter 2 of D.A. Andrews and James Bonta, The Psychology of Criminal Conduct, 5th ed. (New Providence, NJ: Anderson Publishing, 2010) (hereinafter "The Psychology of Criminal Conduct").

[30] Francis T. Cullen and Cheryl Lero Jonson, "Rehabilitation and Treatment Programs," in Crime and Public Policy, ed. James Q. Wilson and Joan Petersilia, 2nd ed. (New York: Oxford University Press, 2011), p. 319.

[31] Ibid.

[32] Vera Institute of Justice's memorandum re: risk and needs assessment, p. 2.

[33] The Psychology of Criminal Conduct, p. 47.

[34] The Role of Offender Risk Assessment, p. 209.
[35] The Psychology of Criminal Conduct, p. 49.
[36] Ibid., p. 49.
[37] Ibid., pp. 49-50.
[38] Ibid., p. 55.
[39] Ibid., p. 60.
[40] Ibid., p. 48.
[41] Ibid.
[42] Vera Institute of Justice's memorandum re: risk and needs assessment, p. 2.
[43] James Bonta and D.A. Andrews, Risk—Need—Responsivity Model for Offender Assessment and Rehabilitation, Public Safety Canada, June 2007, pp. 9-12, http://www.publicsafety.gc.ca/cnt/rsrcs/pblctns/rsk-nd-rspnsvty/index-eng.aspx, hereinafter, "RNR Model for Offender Assessment and Rehabilitation."
[44] R. Karl Hanson, "The Psychological Assessment of Risk for Crime and Violence," Canadian Psychology, vol. 50, no. 3 (2009), p. 172.
[45] James Austin, "The Proper and Improper Use of Risk Assessment in Corrections," Federal Sentencing Reporter, vol. 16, no. 3, February 2004, p. 3 (hereinafter, "The Proper and Improper Use of Risk Assessment in Corrections").
[46] David J. Cook and Christine Michie, "Limitations of Diagnostic Precision and Predictive Utility in the Individual Case: A Challenge for Forensic Practice," Law and Human Behavior, vol. 34, 2010, p. 259 (hereinafter, "Limitations of Diagnostic Precision and Predictive Utility in the Individual Case").
[47] Ibid., p. 271.
[48] Jennifer L. Skeem and John Monahan, Current Directions in Violence Risk Assessment, University of Virginia Law School, Public Law and Legal Theory Research Paper Series, no. 2011-13, March 2011, pp. 8-9.
[49] Ibid.
[50] Limitations of Diagnostic Precision and Predictive Utility in the Individual Case, p. 271.
[51] Stephen D. Gottfredson and Laura J. Moriarty, "Statistical Risk Assessment: Old Problems and New Applications," Crime and Delinquency, vol. 52, no. 1, January 2006, p. 191 (hereinafter "Statistical Risk Assessment: Old Problems and New Applications").
[52] Christopher Baird, A Question of Evidence: A Critique of Risk Assessment Models Used in the Justice System, National Council of Crime and Delinquency, February 2009, p. 3 (hereinafter "A Question of Evidence").
[53] Ibid.
[54] Ibid.
[55] Statistical Risk Assessment: Old Problems and New Applications, p. 191.
[56] A Question of Evidence, p. 3.
[57] Ibid., p. 5.
[58] Statistical Risk Assessment: Old Problems and New Applications, p. 192.
[59] Kelly Hannah-Moffat, Actuarial Sentencing: An "Unsettled" Proposition, paper presented at University at Albany Symposium on Sentencing, September 2010, p. 16 (hereinafter "Actuarial Sentencing: An 'Unsettled' Proposition").
[60] Ibid., p. 14.
[61] Ibid., p. 17.
[62] Michael Tonry, "Legal and Ethical Issues in the Prediction of Recidivism," Federal Sentencing Reporter, vol. 26, no. 3, February 2014, p. 171.
[63] The Psychology of Criminal Conduct, p. 333.

[64] Jay P. Singh and Seena Fazel, "Forensic Risk Assessment: a Metareview," Criminal Justice and Behavior, vol. 37, no. 9, September 2010, p.978.

[65] See, for example, S. 467, S. 2123, H.R. 759, and H.R. 2944.

[66] The Psychology of Criminal Conduct, p. 48.

[67] Ibid.

[68] Vera Institute of Justice's memorandum re: risk and needs assessment, p. 2.

[69] See, for example, H.R. 759.

[70] See, for example, S. 467 and S. 2123.

[71] See, for example, S. 467 and S. 2123.

[72] See, for example, S. 467, S. 2123, H.R. 759, and H.R. 2944.

[73] The Administrative Office of the U.S. Courts reports that in 2012 the average annual cost of probation supervision was $3,347 per probationer, compared to $28,948 to house an inmate in a federal prison. Administrative Office of the U.S. Courts, "Supervision Costs Significantly Less than Incarceration in Federal System," July 18, 2013, http://news.uscourts.gov/supervision-costs-significantly-less-incarceration-federal-system.

[74] Jordan M. Hyatt, Mark H. Bergstrom, and Steven L. Chanenson, "Follow the Evidence: Integrate Risk Assessment into Sentencing," Federal Sentencing Reporter, vol. 23, no. 4, April 2011, pp. 266-268.

[75] Seena Fazel, Jay P. Singh, and Helen Doll, "Use of Risk Assessment Instruments to Predict Violence and Antisocial Behaviour in 73 Samples Involving 24,827 People: Systematic Review and Meta-analysis," BMJ: British Medical Journal, vol. 345, July 24, 2012, http://www.bmj.com/content/bmj/345/bmj.e4692.full.pdf.

[76] Ibid., p. 4.

[77] Letter from Jonathan J. Wroblewski, Director, Office of Policy and Legislation, Criminal Division, U.S. Department of Justice, to The Honorable Patti B. Saris, Chair, U.S. Sentencing Commission, July 29, 2014.

[78] See, for example, S. 467, S. 2123, H.R. 759, and H.R. 2944.

[79] Anne Morrison Piehl and Bert Useem, "Prisons," in Crime and Public Policy, ed. Joan Petersilia and James Q. Wilson, 2nd ed. (New York: Oxford University Press, 2011), p. 542.

[80] Doris Layton MacKenzie, "Reducing the Criminal Activities of Known Offenders and Delinquents: Crime Prevention in the Courts and Corrections," in Evidence-based Crime Prevention, ed. Lawrence W. Sherman, David P. Farrington, Brandon C. Welsh, and Doris Layton MacKenzie (New York: Routledge, 2002), p. 337.

[81] Bert Useem and Anne Morrison Piehl, Prison State: The Challenge of Mass Incarceration (New York: Cambridge University Press, 2008), p. 74.

[82] The Psychology of Criminal Conduct, p. 433.

[83] Ibid., pp. 443-447.

[84] Ibid., p. 451.

[85] As defined at 18 U.S.C. §2332b(g)(5).

[86] As defined at 18 U.S.C. §16.

[87] As described in 42 U.S.C. §16911.

[88] As defined at 18 U.S.C. §1962.

[89] As defined at 21 U.S.C. §848.

[90] As defined at 42 U.S.C. §17601.

[91] As defined at 18 U.S.C. §2332b(g)(5).

[92] As defined at 18 U.S.C. §16.

[93] As described in 42 U.S.C. §16911.

[94] As defined at 21 U.S.C. §848.

[95] As defined at 42 U.S.C. §17601.

[96] "High-level drug offenses" means offenses under section 401(a) of the Controlled Substances Act (21 U.S.C. 841(a)), relating to manufacturing or distributing a controlled substance, but only in the case of a conviction for an offense described in subparagraphs (A), (B), or (C) of subsection (b) of that section for which death or serious bodily injury resulted from the use of such substance.

[97] Only in cases where it was shown beyond a reasonable doubt that the inmate had the intent to cause death and death resulted.

[98] As defined at 18 U.S.C. §2332b(g)(5).

[99] As described in section 111 of the Sex Offender Registration and Notification Act (Title I of the Adam Walsh Child Protection and Safety Act of 2006 (P.L. 109-248)).

[100] For more information on BOP's inmate disciplinary program see CRS Report R42486, The Bureau of Prisons (BOP): Operations and Budget, by Nathan James.

In: Risk Assessment and Sentencing … ISBN: 978-1-63484-561-8
Editor: Julia Campbell

Chapter 2

SENTENCING REFORM: COMPARISON OF SELECTED PROPOSALS*

Jared P. Cole and Charles Doyle

SUMMARY

This is a comparison of selected criminal sentencing reform bills as introduced: H.R. 3713, H.R. 2944, S. 502, and H.R. 920; and S. 2123 as passed by the Senate Judiciary Committee with a manager's amendment. It consists of narrative and charts comparing the bills with respect to adjustments in the mandatory minimum sentencing provisions that apply to controlled substance and firearms offenses, the safety valve, and retroactive application of the Fair Sentencing Act (FSA).

INTRODUCTION

Within a week of each other, Senator Grassley and Representative Goodlatte, respective chairmen of the Senate and House Judiciary Committees, introduced parallel sentencing reform bills with bipartisan cosponsors.[1] By and large in identical language, the two would amend existing mandatory minimum sentence provisions found in federal drug and firearms

* This is an edited, reformatted and augmented version of a Congressional Research Service publication R44246, prepared for Members and Committees of Congress, dated October 26, 2015.

laws. The differences between S. 2123 and H.R. 3713, occasioned by the manager's amendment adopted before the Senate Judiciary Committee passed S. 2123, are noted in the prefatory remarks for each chart, and in the remarks relating to the inventory of federal crimes. The subjects of their proposals appear in earlier proposals including (1) H.R. 2944, which Representatives Sensenbrenner and Scott, the chairman and ranking minority member of the House Judiciary Committee's crime subcommittee, respectively, introduced for themselves and others, and (2) S. 502/H.R. 920, introduced by Senator Lee and Representative Labrador with additional bipartisan cosponsors. Their common components notwithstanding, the bills have some varying features.

MANDATORY MINIMUMS

Controlled Substances

The Controlled Substances Act and the Controlled Substances Import and Export Act establish a series of mandatory minimum sentences for violations of their prohibitions.[2] Trafficking—that is, importing, exporting, or manufacturing, growing, possessing with the intent to distribute—a very substantial amount of various highly addictive substances, such as more than 10 grams of LSD (§841(b)(1)(A)), is punishable by imprisonment for not less than 10 years or more than life.[3] When substantial but lesser amounts are involved, such as 1 gram of LSD (§841(b)(1)(B)), sentences of imprisonment for not less than 5 years or more than life are called for, and imprisonment for not less than 10 years or more than life in the case of a subsequent conviction.[4]

Penalties for both sets of offenses increase if the crime results in a death or if the defendant has a prior conviction for a drug felony.[5]

The proposed amendments are noted and compared in *Table 1*. S. 502/H.R. 920 would reduce the mandatory minimum for the high volume §841(b)(1)(A) and §960(b)(1) offenses to imprisonment for not less than 5 years from not less than 10 years, and the mandatory minimums for the medium volume §841(b)(1)(B) and §960(b)(1) offenses to not less than 2 years from not less than 5 years.[6]

H.R. 2944 would eliminate the mandatory minimum for the high volume §841(b)(1)(A) and §960(b)(1) offenses, except when the defendant was the organizer or leader of a 5 member or more drug enterprise. It would eliminate as well the mandatory minimum for the medium volume §841(b)(1)(B) and §960(b)(2) offenses, except when the defendant was the organizer, leader, manager, or supervisor of a 5 or more member drug enterprise.[7] Moreover, the recidivist enhancement would only come into play when the prior conviction for an offense carrying a maximum penalty of imprisonment for 10 years or more; resulting in a sentence of imprisonment for 13 months or more; and from which the defendant had been released within 10 years of the commission of the subsequent drug offense.[8] H.R. 2944 would allow the court to treat each of its amendments, here and throughout the course of the bill, as grounds for reduced sentencing, on the motion of the court, the defendant, the prosecutor, or the Bureau of Prisons.[9]

S. 2123/H.R. 3713 would create a mini-safety valve to reduce the mandatory minimum for the high volume §841(b)(1)(A) and §960(b)(1) offenses to imprisonment for not less than 5 years, unless the offender had used violence in the commission of the offense; had acted as a supervisor or leader of a drug enterprise; sold to minors; failed to fully reveal all the information or evidence at his disposal relating to the offense or related offenses; and had no prior serious drug or violent felony convictions.[10]

S. 2123/H.R. 3713 would both expand and contract drug recidivist mandatory minimums under the high volume and medium §§841(b)(1)(A), 841(b)(1)(B), 960(b)(1), and 960(b)(2) offenses. Under existing law, any prior drug felony conviction triggers the enhanced recidivist mandatory minimum.[11] Under S. 2123/H.R. 3713, only drug convictions carrying a maximum penalty of 10 years or more and resulting in a sentence of a year or more would trigger the increased recidivist mandatory minimums.[12] On the other hand, convictions for kidnapping, burglary, arson or other serious violent crimes would also serve as a basis for the recidivist mandatory minimums.[13]

The bills would allow the courts, on their own motion or that of the defendant or the Bureau of Prisons, to resentence defendants, convicted prior to S. 2123/H.R. 3713's enactment, as though the bills' reduced recidivist mandatory minimums were in place at the time of prior sentencing. In doing so, the courts would be compelled to consider: the nature and seriousness of the risks to an individual or the community; the defendant's conduct following his initial sentencing; and the statutory sentencing factors which they must ordinarily weigh before imposing punishment.[14]

S. 2123, but not H.R. 3713, would make it clear that resentencing proceedings would be subject to the victims' rights provisions of 18 U.S.C. 3771, and that an inquiry into facts and circumstances associated with the initial sentencing would be a prerequisite to consideration of a resentencing motion.[15] Section 3771 assures victims of the rights "to reasonable, accurate, and timely notice of any public court proceeding, involving the crime ..." and "to the right to be reasonably heard at any public proceeding in the district court involving ... sentencing ..."[16]

H.R. 3713, but not S. 2123, would insist on a sentence of imprisonment for not more than 5 years to be added to, and to be served after, any sentence imposed for the drug trafficking, exporting, or importing offenses, when heroin or fentanyl are involved.[17]

In addition, H.R. 2944 provides that no person shall be sentenced to enhanced punishment under the Controlled Substances Act if the conviction was for possession of a controlled substance, was classified as a misdemeanor in the relevant jurisdiction, or the conviction has been set aside.[18] Further, the government bears the burden of proof in proving beyond a reasonable doubt the existence of the prior conviction.[19]

Table 1. Mandatory Minimum Terms of Imprisonment: Controlled Substances

Offense	Present Law	S. 2123/ H.R. 3713	S. 2123/ H.R. 2944	S. 502/ H.R. 920
I. Trafficking: §841(b)(1)(A)/ §960(b)(1) substances (e.g. 1 kilo + of heroin)	not less than 10 years or more than life	not less than 10 years or more than life but not less than 5 years if: nonviolent; low-level; all info to gov't; no sale to minors; no serious drug/violent felony priors H.R. 3713only: add consecutive sentence of not more than 5 years if heroin or fentanyl	not less than 10 years or more than life (mandatory minimum applies only if leader of 5 ormore) [retroactive]	not less than 5 years or more than life
if death or serious injury results	not less than 20 years or more than life	H.R. 3713only: add consecutive sentence of not more than 5 years if heroin or fentanyl	not less than 20 years or more than life(mandatory minimum applies only if leader of 5 or more) [retroactive]	no change
with one prior	not less than	not lessthan 15	not less than 20 years	not less than

Offense	**Present Law**	**S. 2123/ H.R. 3713**	**S. 2123/ H.R. 2944**	**S. 502/ H.R. 920**
felony drug conviction	20 years or more than life	years or more than life only if prior is serious drug/violent felony [retroactive] H.R. 3713only: add consecutive sentence of not more than 5 years if heroin or fentanyl	or more than life -if prior committed w/i 10 years; penalty for prior was 10 years or more; prior resulted in imprisonment for 13 months or more (mandatory minimum applies only if leader of 5 or more) [retroactive]	10years or more than life
with one prior felony drug conviction and death or serious injury results	life	no change	life -if prior committed w/i 10 years; penalty for prior was 10 years or more; prior resulted in imprisonment for 13 months or more (mandatory minimum applies only if leader of 5 or more) [retroactive]	no change
with two or more prior felony drug convictions	life	not less than 25 years or more than life only if priors are serious drug/violent felony [retroactive]	life-if prior committed w/i 10 years; penalty for prior was 10 years or more; prior resulted in imprisonment for 13 months or more (mandatory minimum applies only if leader of 5 or more) [retroactive]	not less than 25years
II. Trafficking: §841(b)(1)(B)/§ 960(b)(2) substance (e.g. 100g + of heroin)	not less than 5 years or more than 40 years	H.R. 3713 only: add consecutive sentence of notmore than 5 years if heroin or fentanyl	not less than 5 years or more than 40 years (mandatory minimum applies only if the leader or supervisor of 5 or more) [retroactive]	not less than 2years or more than 40 years

Table 1. (Continued)

Offense	Present Law	S. 2123/ H.R. 3713	S. 2123/ H.R. 2944	S. 502/ H.R. 920
if death or serious injury results	not less than 20 years or more than life	H.R. 3713 only: add consecutive sentence of not more than 5 years if heroin or fentanyl	not less than 20 years or more than life (mandatory minimum applies only if the leader or supervisor of 5 or more) [retroactive]	no change
with one prior felony drug conviction	not less than 10 years or more than life	not less 10 years or more than life only if prior is serious drug/violent felony [retroactive] H.R. 3713 only: add consecutive sentence of not more than 5 years if heroin or fentanyl	not less than 10 years or more than life if prior committed w/i 10 years; penalty for prior was 10 years or more; prior resulted in imprisonment for 13 months or more (mandatory minimum applies only if the leader or supervisor of 5 ormore) [retroactive]	not less than 5years or more than life
with one prior felony drug conviction and death or serious injury results	life	no change	if prior committed w/i 10 years; penalty for prior was 10 years or more; prior resulted in imprisonment for 13 months or more (mandatory minimum applies only if the leader or supervisor of 5 or more)[retroactive]	no change
III. Trafficking: §841(b)(1)(C)/ §960(b)(3), except per (b)(1)(A), (B), or (D), sch. I or II drugs, GHB, or 1 gram of Rohypnol	not more than 20 years	H.R. 3713 only: add consecutive sentence of not more than 5 years if heroin or fentanyl	only if type and quantity of (b)(1)(A) or (B) substances and part of 5or moremember trafficking group but not a leader or supervisor	no change

Offense	Present Law	S. 2123/ H.R. 3713	S. 2123/ H.R. 2944	S. 502/ H.R. 920
if death or serious injury results	not less than 20 years or more than life	H.R. 3713 only: add consecutive sentence of not more than 5 years ifheroin or fentanyl	only if type and quantity of (b)(1)(A) or (B) substances and part of 5 or more member trafficking group but not a leader or supervisor [retroactive]	no change

Source: CRS from S. 2123, H.R. 3713, H.R. 2944, S. 502, and H.R. 920.

Safety Valve

The so-called safety valve provision of 18 U.S.C. 3553(f) allows a court to sentence qualified defendants below the statutory mandatory minimum in controlled substance trafficking and possession cases.[20] To qualify, a defendant may not have used violence in the course of the offense.[21] He must not have played a managerial role in the offense if it involved group participation.[22] The offense must not have resulted in a death or serious bodily injury.[23] The defendant must make full disclosure of his involvement in the offense, providing the government with all the information and evidence at his disposal.[24] Finally, the defendant must have an almost spotless criminal record, that is, not more than 1 criminal history point.[25]

Criminal history points and categories are a feature of the U.S. Sentencing Commission's Sentencing Guidelines. The Guidelines assign points based on the sentences imposed for prior state and federal convictions. For example, the Guidelines assign 1 point for any past conviction that resulted in a sentence of less than 60 days incarceration; 2 points for any conviction resulting in a sentence of incarceration for at least 60 days; and 3 points for any conviction resulting in a sentence of incarceration of more than a year and a month.[26]

The Sentencing Commission's report on mandatory minimum sentences suggested that Congress consider expanding safety valve eligibility to defendants with 2 or possibly 3 criminal history points.[27] The report indicated that under the Guidelines a defendant's criminal record "can have a disproportionate and excessively severe cumulative sentencing impact on certain drug offenders."[28] The Commission explained that the Guidelines are construed to ensure that the sentence they recommend in a given case calls for a term of imprisonment that is not less than an applicable mandatory minimum.[29]

In addition, the drug offenses have escalated mandatory minimums for repeat offenders.[30] Moreover, similarly situated drug offenders may be treated differently, because the states punish simple drug possession differently and prosecutors decide when to press recidivism qualifications differently.[31]

S. 502/H.R. 920 would raise the qualification threshold to 3 criminal history points from 1 criminal history point and make no further changes.[32]

H.R. 2944 would expand the safety valve to mandatory minimums associated with the use of firearm during and in furtherance of a drug trafficking cases as well as to drug trafficking mandatory minimums.[33] The bill would also raise the criminal history point threshold to 3 as long as the defendant's prior criminal record did not consist of convictions for violence, firearms, racketeering, terrorism, or sex offenses.[34] H.R. 2944 would also discount convictions that were the product of a reduced, distressed, or coerced state of mind.[35]

S. 2123 and H.R. 3713 would change the safety valve as well. First, a defendant would be safety valve eligible with 3 or fewer criminal history points if he had not been convicted previously of either a drug trafficking offense, a violent offense, or a "3-point offense" (i.e., one for which he was incarcerated for 60 days or more).[36]

Second, the two proposals would permit the court to waive the criminal history disqualification, in cases other than those involving a past serious drug felony or serious violent felony conviction, if it concluded that the defendant's criminal history score overstated the seriousness of his criminal record or the likelihood that he would commit other offenses.[37]

Table 2. Safety Valve

General	**Covered Offenses/ Qualifications**	**S. 2123/ H.R. 3713**	**H.R. 2944**	**S. 502/ H.R. 920**
18 U.S.C. 3553(f): Court may sentence under the USSG w/o regard to the statutory mandatory minimums	Covered offenses.21 U.S.C. 841, 846, 960, 963 (trafficking controlled substances/ attempt)	no change	21 U.S.C. 841, 846, 960, 963 (trafficking controlled substances/attempt) and 18 U.S.C. 924(c)(firearm possession in furtherance) in relation to drug trafficking	no change

General	Covered Offenses/ Qualifications	S. 2123/ H.R. 3713	H.R. 2944	S. 502/ H.R. 920
each prior sentence of less than 60 days = 1 criminal history point each prior sentence of 60 days or up to 13 months = 2 criminal history points each prior sentence of 13 months or more = 3 criminal history points (category I = 0 or 1 point; category II = 2 or 3 points)	(1) no more than 1 criminal history point	no more than 4 criminal history points; but no 3-point prior sentences; no 2-point drug trafficking or violent offense prior convictions court may waive the qualification if it concludes the point total over represents criminal history or prospect of recidivism	no more than 1 criminal history point; OR no more than 3 criminal history points; and no violent, firearms, sex, terrorism, racketeering, or conspiracy to use of invest drug profits convictions; OR offense committed as a result of: mental illness or drug addiction; financial, emotional, or mental distress; combat induced trauma; or direction or coercion of a victim of abuse or domestic violence	no more than 3criminal historypoints
	(2) no use of threats, violence, or firearms	no change	(2) no use of threats or violence	no change
	(3) no resulting death or serious bodily injury	no change	no change	no change
	(4) not a leader or supervisor and not part of §848 (drug kingpin) enterprise	no change	(4) not a leader or supervisor of a group of 5 or more and not part of §848 (drug kingpin) enterprise	no change

Table 2. (Continued)

General	Covered Offenses/ Qualifications	S. 2123/ H.R. 3713	H.R. 2944	S. 502/ H.R. 920
	(5) tell all	no change	information may not be used in USSG calculations	no change

Source: CRS from S. 2123, H.R. 3713, H.R. 2944, S. 502, and H.R. 920.

Firearms

There are two firearms-related offenses that call for the imposition of a mandatory minimum sentence of imprisonment. One, the so-called three strikes provision, also known as the Armed Career Criminal Act (ACCA), imposes a 15-year mandatory minimum sentence on an offender convicted of unlawful possession of a firearm who has three prior convictions for a drug offense or a violent felony.[38] The other, 18 U.S.C. 924(c), imposes one of a series of mandatory terms of imprisonment upon a defendant convicted of the use of a firearm during the course of a drug offense or a crime of violence.[39]

The ACCA limits qualifying state and federal drug offenses to those punishable by imprisonment for more than 10 years.[40] The qualifying federal and state violent felonies are burglary, arson, extortion, the use of explosives, or any other felony which either has the use or threat of physical force as an element.[41] S. 2123 and H.R. 3713 would reduce the mandatory minimum penalty from 15 years to 10 years.[42] They would also make the modification retroactively applicable in the same manner as the proposed mandatory minimum reductions in the case of controlled substances. That is, they would also permit federal courts to reduce the terms of imprisonment of defendants previously sentenced, after considering the defendant's conduct after his initial sentence, "the nature and seriousness of the danger to any person or the community," and the generally applicable sentencing factors of 18 U.S.C. 3553(a).[43] Again, however, H.R. 3713's retroactivity would only apply to defendants without a prior serious violent felony conviction.[44] In contrast, H.R. 2944 does not reduce these mandatory minimum penalties. However, it alters the definition of a "serious drug offense" to one punishable by imprisonment for not more than 10 years, resulting in a sentence of more than 13 months, conviction for which occurred within the last 10 years not counting time in prison.[45] In addition it alters the definition of "violent felony" to require a sentence of imprisonment for 13 months.[46] Further, it provides that an individual may not be sentenced under the provision unless the U.S. Attorney files an information with the court—served on the defendant or counsel—specifying the previous convictions to be relied upon.[47]

Section 924(c) brings firearm mandatory minimum tack-on status to any federal drug felony and to any other federal felony, which either has the use of physical force or threat of physical force as an element or which by its nature involves a substantial risk of the use of physical force.[48]

While the ACCA calls for a single 15-year mandatory minimum, §924(c) imposes one of several different minimum sentences when a firearm is used or possessed in furtherance of another federal crime of violence or of drug trafficking. The mandatory minimums, imposed in addition to the sentence imposed for the underlying crime of violence or drug trafficking, vary depending upon the circumstances:

- imprisonment for not less than 5 years, unless one of the higher mandatory minimums below applies;
- imprisonment for not less than 7 years, if a firearm is brandished;
- imprisonment for not less than 10 years, if a firearm is discharged;
- imprisonment for not less than 10 years, if a firearm is a short-barreled rifle or shotgun or is a semi-automatic weapon;
- imprisonment for not less than 15 years, if the offense involves armor-piercing ammunition;
- imprisonment for not less than 25 years, if the offender has a prior conviction for violation of §924(c);
- imprisonment for not less than 30 years, if the firearm is a machine gun or destructive device or is equipped with a silencer; and
- imprisonment for life, if the offender has a prior conviction for violation of §924(c) and if the firearm is a machine gun or destructive device or is equipped with a silencer.[49]

One of §924(c)'s distinctive features is that its repeat offender provision has been construed to include conviction of an earlier count within the same prosecution.[50] Under this stacking of counts, a defendant convicted of several counts arising out of a single crime spree involving the robbery of several convenience stores, for example, may face a mandatory term of imprisonment of well over 100 years.[51]

S. 2123 and H.R. 3713 would make clear that a conviction must have become final before it could be counted for purposes of enhancing the mandatory minimum.[52] They would also reduce the repeat offender mandatory minimum from imprisonment for not less than 25 years to not less than 15 years.[53] The proposals, however, would expand the repeat offender mandatory minimum to include recidivists with prior violent state crime convictions. And with one exception, they would both permit courts to apply the changes retroactively to cases that had become final, provided they took into account the defendant's post-conviction conduct, the nature and seriousness of threats to individual or community safety, and the generally applicable sentencing factors.[54] H.R. 3713 differs from S. 2123 in one respect. It would not afford retroactive application to a defendant who has a prior conviction for a serious violent felony.[55] S. 2123 differs from H.R. 3713 in one respect. As it would do in case of drug mandatory adjustments, it would make it clear that resentencing proceedings would be subject to the victims' rights provisions of 18 U.S.C. 3771, and that an inquiry into facts and circumstances associated with the initial sentencing would be a prerequisite to consideration of a resentencing motion.[56] Section 3771 assures victims of the rights "to reasonable, accurate, and timely notice of any public court proceeding, involving the crime ..." and "to the right to be reasonably heard at any public proceeding in the district court involving ... sentencing ..."[57]

While H.R. 2944 also requires that a conviction be final to be counted for purposes of enhancing the mandatory minimum, it does not reduce the repeat offender mandatory minimum from imprisonment.[58] In addition, the bill would modify the current statutory trigger's "during and in relation to any crime of violence or drug trafficking crime" language to "not include any possession not on the person of, or within arm's reach and otherwise readily and immediately accessible to the defendant at the time and place of the offense."[59]

S. 2123 and H.R. 3713 each have a third firearms amendment that, although not a strict mandatory minimum amendment, would increase the likelihood of imprisonment by operation of implementing sentencing guidelines by simply increasing the maximum sentence authorized for the offense or offenses.[60] The two bills would increase from imprisonment for not more than 10 years to not more than 15 years the sentences for the following firearms offenses:[61]

- false statements in connection with the purchase of a firearm or ammunition;[62]
- sale of a firearm or ammunition to, or possession by, a convicted felon or other disqualified individual;[63]
- while in the employ of a disqualified individual, receipt or possession of a firearm or ammunition;[64]
- knowing transportation of stolen firearms or ammunition;[65]
- knowing sale, possession, or pledge as security of stolen firearms or ammunition;[66] or
- transfer or possession of a machine gun under certain circumstances.[67] In contrast, H.R. 2944 contains no such provision.

Table 3. Sentencing for Firearms Offenses

Offense	Present Law	S. 2123/ H.R. 3713	H.R. 2944	S. 502/ H.R. 920
I. 18 U.S.C. 924(a)(2) (penalty for §922 firearms offenses)	violations of the following subsections of 18 U.S.C. 922 are punishable by imprisonment for not more than *10 years:*	violations of the following subsections of 18 U.S.C. 922 are punishable by imprisonment for not more than *15 years*:	no change	no change
	(a)(6) false statements in the acquisition of a firearm	no change	no change	no change
	(d) sale of a firearm to an ineligible person	no change	no change	no change
	(g) possession of a firearm by an ineligible person	no change	no change	no change
	(i) interstate transportation of a stolen firearm	no change	no change	no change
	(j) possession of a stolen firearm that has travelled in interstate commerce	no change	no change	no change

Table 3. (Continued)

Offense	Present Law	S. 2123/ H.R. 3713	H.R. 2944	S. 502/ H.R. 920
	(o) unlawful transfer of a machinegun	no change	no change	no change
II. 18 U.S.C. 924(e) (Armed Career Criminal) (3 strikes)	imprisonment for not less than *15 years*for firearm possession by an ineligible person w/ 3 prior violent felony or serious drug convictions	imprisonment for not less than *10 years*for firearm possession by an ineligible person w/ 3 prior violent felony or serious drug convictions [retroactive but H.R. 3713 bars retroactivity when the prior conviction is for a serious violent felony]	no change	no change
	"serious drug offense" = one punishable by imprisonment for not more than 10 years	no change	"serous drug offense" = one punishable by imprisonment for not more than 10 years, resulting a sentence of more than 13 months, conviction for which occurredw/i 10 years (not counting time in prison)	no change
	"violent felony" = burglary, arson, extortion felony or felony with use of physical force element	no change	"violent felony" = burglary, arson, extortion felony or felony with use of physical force element, resulting a sentence of more than 13 months	no change

Offense	**Present Law**	**S. 2123/ H.R. 3713**	**H.R. 2944**	**S. 502/ H.R. 920**
	includes ct. finding of a juvenile involved in a violent felony	no change	includes ct. finding of a juvenile involved in a violent felony, but does not includea finding which occurredmore than 10 years ago (not counting time in prison)	no change
III. Various mandatory minimums for firearm possession associated w/ drug trafficking and violent felony, 18 U.S.C. 924(c)	imprisonment for not less than 25 yearsfor carrying of a firearm during and in relation to, or possession in furtherance of, a crime of violence or drug trafficking offense, in the case of second or subsequent conviction	imprisonment for not less than 15 yearsfor carrying of a firearm during and in relation to, or possession in furtherance of, a crime of violence or drug trafficking offense, in the case of second or subsequent conviction [retroactive; but H.R. 3713 bars retroactivity when the prior conviction is for a serious violent felony]	imprisonment for not less than 25 yearsfor carrying of a firearm during and in relation to, or possession in furtherance of, a crime of violence or drug trafficking offense, in the case of second or subsequent conviction	no change
		no change	"during and in relation to" = possession on the person or within easy reach	no change
	permits treating conviction of successive counts w/I the same prosecution as"second or subsequent convictions"	prior conviction must be final tobe counted [retroactive]	prior conviction must be final to be counted	no change

Source: CRS from S. 2123, H.R. 3713, H.R. 2944, S. 502, and H.R. 920.

Fair Sentencing Act

Originally, the Controlled Substances Act made no distinction between powder cocaine and crack cocaine (cocaine base).[68] The 1986 Anti-Drug Abuse Act introduced a 100-1 sentencing ratio between the two, so that trafficking in 50 grams of crack cocaine carried the same penalties as trafficking in 5,000 grams of powder cocaine.[69] The 2010 Fair Sentencing Act (FSA) replaced it with the present 500-28 ratio, so that trafficking in 280 grams of crack cocaine carries the same penalties as 5,000 grams of powder cocaine.[70] The Sentencing Commission subsequently revised the Sentencing Guidelines to reflect the change and made the modification retroactively applicable at the discretion of the sentencing court.[71]

The FSA reductions apply to cocaine offenses committed thereafter. They also apply to offenses committed beforehand when sentencing occurred after the time of enactment.[72] Federal courts have discretion to reduce a sentence imposed under a Sentencing Guideline that was subsequently substantially reduced.[73] The FSA, however, does not apply to sentences imposed prior to its enactment,[74] and it does not apply in sentence reduction hearings triggered by new Sentencing Guidelines.[75] In such proceedings, the courts remain bound by the mandatory minimums in effect prior to enactment of the FSA.[76]

S. 2123 and H.R. 3713, in roughly the same terms, would change that and would allow a court to reduce a sentence, imposed for an offense committed prior to the FSA, to reflect its provisions, unless the court had already done so or unless the original sentence was imposed consistent with the FSA amendments.[77] H.R. 2944 would simply make the FSA retroactively applicable.[78]

Table 4. Retroactivity of the Fair Sentencing Act

Offense	Present Law	S. 2123/ H.R. 3713	H.R. 2944	S. 502/ H.R. 920
FSA, P.L. 111-220(2010) increased the amounts of crack cocaine need to trigger mandatory minimum sentences	amendments are ordinarily not retroactive	a court may reduce a sentence for pre-FSA offenses to reflect FSA changes on its own motion or that of the	a court may reduce a sentence for pre-FSA offenses to reflect FSA changes on its own motion or that of the defendant,	a court may reduce a sentence for pre-FSA offenses to reflect FSA changes on its own motion or that of the defendant, Bureau of Prisons, or prosecutor,but:

Offense	Present Law	S. 2123/ H.R. 3713	H.R. 2944	S. 502/ H.R. 920
		defendant, Bureau of Prisons, or prosecutor, but:	Bureau of Prisons, or prosecutor	
		court is not required to reduce; and may not if:	no comparable provision	court is not required to reduce; and may notif:
		S. 2123only: the sentence was already imposed or reduced to reflect FSA changes; H.R. 3713only: the sentence already imposed or reduced to a one greater that FSA mandatory minimum; or	no comparable provision	no comparable provision
		a motion under this section to reduce has already been denied; also under H.R. 3713, a motion under FSA to reduce has already been denied	no comparable provision	a motion under this section or FSA to reduce has already been denied

Source: CRS from S. 2123, H.R. 3713, H.R. 2944, S. 502, and H.R. 920.

NEW MANDATORY MINIMUMS

H.R. 3713 and H.R. 2944 would create no new mandatory minimum sentencing provisions. S. 2123, on the other hand, would establish two: one for interstate domestic violence offenses and another for certain violations of the International Emergency Economic Powers Act (IEEPA).

Existing federal law criminalizes interstate domestic violence and interstate stalking, and penalizes them equally. S. 2123 would establish a mandatory minimum sentence of imprisonment for not less than 10 years when death resulted from interstate domestic violence.[79] In addition, it would increase the maximum penalties for interstate domestic violence from imprisonment for not more than 20 years to not more than 25 years when life-threatening or permanent disfigurement resulted and from imprisonment for not more than 10 years to not more than 15 years when a dangerous weapon was used or serious bodily injury resulted.[80] Otherwise, the Senate proposal would leave the penalties for interstate domestic violence and interstate stalking unchanged.

IEEPA authorizes the President to exercise various authorities to "deal with any unusual and extraordinary [overseas threat] ... to the national security, foreign policy or economy of the United States." Presidents have used this authority to issue executive orders banning various unlicensed transactions with various countries, entities, and individuals. IEEPA violations are punishable by imprisonment for not more than 20 years.[81]

S. 2123 would create a separate mandatory minimum sentence of imprisonment for not less than five years for three types of IEEPA violations. One prohibits IEEPA violations that involve providing defense articles or services as defined by the Arms Export Control Act to countries under an arms embargo.[82] Another prohibits IEEPA violations that involve supplying goods or services for the foreign development of weapons of mass destruction.[83] The third prohibits IEEPA violations that furnish certain foreign entities with goods and services that are subject to export restrictions.[84]

In contrast, H.R. 2944 does not create new mandatory minimum sentences for crimes.

INVENTORY OF FEDERAL CRIMES

S. 2123 would call for an inventory of federal crimes. Section 109 of the bill would direct the Attorney General to prepare and provide the House and Senate Committees on the Judiciary an inventory of federal statutory crimes and of federal regulatory offenses. The compilation of federal statutory crimes would have to identify for each offense: the attendant penalties and mens rea; the number of referrals for prosecution, prosecutions, convictions, and sentences imposed; as well as the number of prosecutions which did not require proof of a mens rea.[85] The compilation of federal regulatory offenses would be organized by enforcing agency and would require the same information for regulatory offenses as required for statutory offenses.[86] The Attorney General and pertinent agency head would also be responsible for the creation of a publicly available online index of such offenses.[87] Similarly, H.R. 2944 requires the Attorney General to produce and publish a list of "the various Federal law violations that carry criminal penalties."[88] In addition, federal agencies must obtain the Attorney General's approval to add a criminal penalty to an agency regulation.[89] Finally, the Attorney General must develop procedures to provide coordination between the Department of Justice and other federal agencies to determine whether criminal or civil penalties are most appropriate to address unlawful conduct that involves federal agencies; and to coordinate between federal and state law enforcement officers to reduce duplicative prosecutions.[90]

End Notes

[1] S. 2123, H.R. 3713.

[2] Portions of this report have been borrowed from earlier reports on mandatory minimum sentencing by Charles Doyle.

[3] 21 U.S.C. 841(b)(1)(A); 21 U.S.C. 960(b)(1). The threshold amounts covered by the sections are "(i) 1 kilogram or more of a mixture or substance containing a detectable amount of heroin; (ii) 5 kilograms or more of a mixture or substance containing a detectable amount of- (I) coca leaves, except coca leaves and extracts of coca leaves from which cocaine, ecgonine, and derivatives of ecgonine or their salts have been removed; (II) cocaine, its salts, optical and geometric isomers, and salts of isomers; (III) ecgonine, its derivatives, their salts, isomers, and salts of isomers; or (IV) any compound, mixture, or preparation which contains any quantity of any of the substances referred to in subclauses (I) through (III); (iii) 280 grams or more of a mixture or substance described in clause (ii) which contains cocaine base; (iv) 100 grams or more of phencyclidine (PCP) or 1 kilogram or more of a mixture or substance containing a detectable amount of phencyclidine (PCP); (v) 10 grams or more of a mixture or substance containing a detectable amount of lysergic acid diethylamide (LSD); (vi) 400 grams or more of a mixture or substance containing a detectable amount of N-phenyl-N- [1- (2-phenylethyl) -4-piperidinyl] propanamide or 100 grams or more of a mixture or substance containing a detectable amount of any analogue of N-phenyl-N-[1-(2-phenylethyl)-4-piperidinyl] propanamide; (vii) 1,000 kilograms or more of a mixture or substance containing a detectable amount of marihuana, or 1,000 or more marihuana plants regardless of weight; or (viii) 50 grams or more of methamphetamine, its salts, isomers, and salts of its isomers or 500 grams or more of a mixture or substance containing a detectable amount of methamphetamine, its salts, isomers, or salts of its isomers." 21 U.S.C. 841(b)(1)(ii)-(vii).

[4] 21 U.S.C. 841(b)(1)(A), 841(b)(1)(B), 960(b)(1), 960(b)(2). The threshold amounts for the substances in §841(b)(1)(A) are 10 times the threshold amounts for those in §841(b)(1)(B), e.g., for heroin,1,000 grams (1 kilogram) v.100 grams. The same ratio applies in the case of exporting or importing these substances, §§960(b)(1), 960(b)(2).

[5] 21 U.S.C. 841(b)(1)(A), 841(b)(1)(B), 960(b)(1), 960(b)(2).

[6] S. 502/H.R. 920, §4(a)(2)(A)(i), 4(b)(1)(C), proposed 21 U.S.C. 841(b)(1)(A), 841(b)(1)(B), 960(b)(1), (960(b)(2).

[7] H.R. 2944, §401(a), 4(c), proposed 21 U.S.C. 841(i), 960(e).

[8] H.R. 2944, §403(a), (b), proposed 21 U.S.C. 802(44), (57).

[9] H.R. 2944, §405, proposed 18 U.S.C. 3582(c)(3)("[I]n the case of a defendant who was sentenced to a term of imprisonment for an offense for which the minimum or maximum term of imprisonment was subsequently reduced as a result of the amendments made by the Sensenbrenner-Scott SAFE Justice Reinvestment Act of 2015, upon motion of the defendant, counsel for the defendant, counsel for the Government, or the Director of the Bureau of Prisons, or, on its own motion, the court may reduce the term of imprisonment consistent with that reduction, after considering the factors set forth in subsections (a) and (d) through (g) of section 3553 to the extent applicable. If the court does grant a sentence reduction, the reduced sentence shall not be less than permitted under current statutory law. If the court denies a motion made under this paragraph, the movant may file another motion under this subsection, not earlier than 5 years after each denial, which may be granted if the offender demonstrates the offender's compliance with recidivism-reduction programming or other efforts the offender has undertaken to improve the likelihood of successful re-entry and decrease any risk to public safety posed by the defendant's release").

[10] S. 2123, §103(a)/H.R. 3713, §4(a), proposed 18 U.S.C. 3553(i). A "serious drug felony" would be a state or federal offense for which the maximum penalty is imprisonment for not more than 10 years and which resulted in a sentence of imprisonment for more than 1 year. A "serious violent felony" is an offense which resulted in a sentence of imprisonment for more than 1 year and is either an assault as described in 18 U.S.C. 113 or an offense described in 18 U.S.C. 3559(c)(2)(F). Under 18 U.S.C. 3559(c)(2)(F), "'serious violent felony' means - (i) a Federal or State offense, by whatever designation and wherever committed, consisting of murder (as described in section 1111); manslaughter other than involuntary manslaughter (as described in section 1112); ... aggravated sexual abuse and sexual abuse (as described in sections 2241 and 2242); abusive sexual contact (as described in sections 2244(a)(1) and (a)(2)); kidnapping; aircraft piracy (as described in section 46502 of Title 49); robbery (as described in section 2111, 2113, or 2118); carjacking (as described in section 2119); extortion; arson; firearms use; firearms possession (as described in section 924(c)); or attempt, conspiracy, or solicitation to commit any of the above offenses; and (ii) any other offense punishable by a maximum term of imprisonment of 10 years or more that has as an element the use, attempted use, or threatened use of physical force against the person of another or that, by its nature, involves a substantial risk that physical force against the person of another may be used in the course of committing the offense."

[11] 21 U.S.C. 841(b)(1)(A), 841(b)(1)(B), 802(44).

[12] S. 2123, §101(a)(1), (2), 101(b)(1), (2)/H.R. 3713, §2(a)(1), (2), 2(b)(1),(2); proposed 21 U.S.C. 841(b)(1)(A),

841(b)(1)(B), 960(b)(1), 960(b)(2), 802(57).

[13] S. 2123, §101(a)(1), (2), 101(b)(1), (2)/H.R. 3713, §2(a)(1), (2), 2(b)(1),(2); proposed 21 U.S.C. 841(b)(1)(A),

841(b)(1)(B), 960(b)(1), 960(b)(2), 802(58).

[14] S. 2123, §101(c)(2), H.R. 3713, §2(c)(2). H.R. 3713 alone would preclude retroactive application where the prior offense is a serious violent felony. It is unclear what impact this would have since the bills make serious violent felonies trigger offenses when they would have been when the pre-bill sentence was imposed.

[15] S. 2123, §101(c)(2).

[16] 18 U.S.C. 3771(a)(2), (4).

[17] H.R. 3713, §2(a)(3), 2(b)(3); proposed 21 U.S.C. 841(a)(8), (9), 960(b)(8), (b)(9).

[18] H.R. 2944 §403(f).

[19] H.R. 2944 §403(f).

[20] 18 U.S.C. 3553(f)(" Notwithstanding any other provision of law, in the case of an offense under section 401, 404, or 406 of the Controlled Substances Act (21 U.S.C. 841, 844, 846) or section 1010 or 1013 of the Controlled Substances Import and Export Act (21 U.S.C. 960, 963), the court shall impose a sentence pursuant to guidelines promulgated by the United States Sentencing Commission under section 994 of title 28 without regard to any statutory minimum sentence, if the court finds at sentencing, after the Government has been afforded the opportunity to make a recommendation ..."). See, generally, CRS Report R41326, Federal Mandatory Minimum Sentences: The Safety Valve and Substantial Assistance Exceptions, by Charles Doyle.

[21] 18 U.S.C. 3553(f)(2)("... if the court finds at sentencing ... that ... (2) the defendant did not use violence or credible threats of violence or possess a firearm or other dangerous weapon (or induce another participant to do so) in connection with the offense").

[22] 18 U.S.C. 3553(f)(4)("... if the court finds at sentencing ... that ... (4) the defendant was not an organizer, leader, manager, or supervisor of others in the offense, as determined under the sentencing guidelines and was not engaged in a continuing criminal enterprise, as defined in section 408 of the Controlled Substances Act").

[23] 18 U.S.C. 3553(f)(3)("... if the court finds at sentencing ... that ... (3) the offense did not result in death or serious bodily injury to any person").

[24] 18 U.S.C. 3553(f)(5)("... if the court finds at sentencing ... that ... (5) not later than the time of the sentencing hearing, the defendant has truthfully provided to the Government all information and evidence the defendant has concerning the offense or offenses that were part of the same course of conduct or of a common scheme or plan, but the fact that the defendant has no relevant or useful other information to provide or that the Government is already aware of the information shall not preclude a determination by the court that the defendant has complied with this requirement").

[25] 18 U.S.C. 3553(f)(1)("... if the court finds at sentencing ... that - (1) the defendant does not have more than 1 criminal history point, as determined under the sentencing guidelines").

[26] U.S.S.G. §4A1.1.

[27] United States Sentencing Commission, Report to the Congress: Mandatory Minimum Penalties in the Federal Criminal Justice System, 355 (Oct. 2011).

[28] Id. at 352.

[29] Id.

[30] Id.

[31] Id. at 353 ("Interviews of prosecutors and defense attorneys in 13 districts confirm that different districts have adopted different practices with respect to filing the necessary information required to seek an enhanced penalty under 21 U.S.C. §851[relating to proof of a prior conviction] in part because of its severity. The structure of the recidivist provisions in 21 U.S.C. §§841 and 960 fosters inconsistent application, in part, because their applicability turns on the varying statutory maximum penalties for state drug offenses").

[32] S. 502/H.R. 920, §2, proposed 18 U.S.C. 3553(f)(1).

[33] H.R. 2944, §402(a)(1), proposed 18 U.S.C. 3553(f).

[34] H.R. 2944, §402(a)(2); proposed 18 U.S.C. 3553(f)(1)(A), (B) would read: "(1) the defendant – (A) does not have a criminal history category higher than I after any downward departure under the sentencing guidelines; (B) does not have – (i) a criminal history category higher than II after any downward departure under the sentencing guidelines; (ii) any prior conviction for an offense that has as an element the use, attempted use, or threatened use of physical force against the person of another; and (iii) the offense of conviction that is – (I) an offense under section 922 or 924; (II) a sex offense (as defined in section 111 of the Adam Walsh Child Protection and Safety Act of 2006); (III) a Federal crime of terrorism (as defined in section 2332b(g)(5)); (IV) a racketeering offense under section 1962; or (V) conspiring to use and invest illicit drug profits under section 414 of the Controlled Substances Act."

[35] H.R. 2944, §402(a)(2); proposed 18 U.S.C. 3553(f)(1)(C)("committed the offense as the result of – (i) mental illness, cognitive deficits, or a history of persistent or serious substance abuse or addiction; (ii) financial, emotional, or mental distress; (iii) trauma suffered while serving on active duty in an armed conflict zone for a branch of the United States military; or (iv) victimization stemming from any combination of physical, mental, emotional, or psychological abuse or domestic violence, if the offense was committed at the direction of another individual who – (I) was a more culpable participant in the instant offense or played a significantly greater role in the offense; or (II) effectively coerced the defendant's involvement in the offense by means of threats or abuse either personally or from any person or group").

[36] S. 2123, §102(a)(1); H.R. 3713, §3(1); proposed 18 U.S.C. 3553(f)(1). They would define "drug trafficking offense" for these purposes as a state, federal, or foreign drug trafficking offense without reference to the attendant penalties; it would define "violent offense" as a crime punishable by imprisonment which is described in 18 U.S.C. 16 (i.e., a crime one of whose elements is the use or threat of physical force or a felony that by its nature involves a substantial risk of the use of physical force), S. 2123, §102(a)(2); H.R. 3713, §2(a)(2), proposed 18 U.S.C. 3553(h).

[37] S. 2123, §§102(a)(2), 101(a)(1); H.R. 3713, §§3(a)(2), 2(a)(1); proposed 18 U.S.C. 3553(g)(1).

[38] 18 U.S.C. 924(e). See, generally, CRS Report R41449, Armed Career Criminal Act (18 U.S.C. 924(e)): An Overview, by Charles Doyle.

[39] See, generally, CRS Report R41412, Federal Mandatory Minimum Sentencing: The 18 U.S.C. 924(c) Tack-On in Cases Involving Drugs or Violence, by Charles Doyle.

[40] 18 U.S.C. 924(e)(2)(A).

[41] 18 U.S.C. 924(e)(2)(B). The statute includes a third category of violent felonies: that is, crimes like the enumerated crimes (burglary, arson, etc.) which present a serious potential risk of physical injury, 18 U.S.C. 924(e)(2)(B)(ii). The Supreme Court recently held this third category unconstitutionally vague and an impermissible bases for imposition of an enhanced sentence under §924(e), Johnson v. United States, 135 S. Ct. 2551, 2563 (2015).

[42] S. 2123, §105(a)(2); H.R. 3713, §6(a)(2); proposed 18 U.S.C. 924(e)(1).

[43] S. 2123, §105(c)(2); H.R. 3713, §6(b)(2).

[44] H.R. 3713, §§6(b)(2), 2(a)(1).

[45] H.R. 2944 §403(c).

[46] H.R. 2944 §403(c).

[47] H.R. 2944 §403(d).

[48] 18 U.S.C. 924(c)(2), (3).

[49] 18 U.S.C. 924(c)(1), (5).

[50] E.g., United States v. Penny, 576 F.3d 297, 316 (6th Cir. 2009)("[W]hen two separate predicate offenses for triggering §924(c)(1) are charged and proved, a defendant may be convicted and sentenced for two separate crimes, even if both offenses were committed in the course of the same event"); United States v. Sandstrom, 594 F.3d 634, 658 (8th Cir. 2010)("[M]ultiple underlying offenses support multiple §924(c) convictions").

[51] E.g., United States v. Richardson, 793 F.3d 612, 633 (6th Cir. 2015)("We have regularly upheld sentences exceeding 1, 494 months for §924(c) violations related to armed robberies").

[52] S. 2123, §104(a)(1); H.R. 3713, §5(a)(1); proposed 18 U.S.C. 924(c)(1)(C). The provision would read: "(C) in the case of a violation of this subsection that occurs after a prior conviction under this subsection or under State law for a crime of violence that contains as an element of the offense the carrying, brandishing, or use of a firearm has become final."

[53] S. 2123, §104(a)(2); H.R. 3713, §5(a)(2); proposed 18 U.S.C. 924(c)(1)(C)(i).

[54] S. 2123, §104(b)(2); H.R. 3713, §5(b)(2).

[55] H.R. 3713, §5(b)(2).

[56] S. 2123, §§104(b)(2), 105(b)(2).

[57] 18 U.S.C. 3771(a)(2), (4).

[58] H.R. 2944 §421.

[59] H.R. 2944 §421.

[60] The maximum penalty which Congress assigns to a crime is one mark of how serious Congress considers the offense. The Sentencing Guidelines are designed to ensure that comparable offenders receive comparable punishment, U.S.S.G. ch.1, pt. A, 3. When Congress increases the maximum penalty assigned to a crime, the Sentencing Commission would ordinarily adjust the pertinent sentencing guideline to reflect the appropriate increased level of severity, and thereby increase the likelihood of sentencing range that would require imprisonment.

[61] S. 2123, §105(a)(1); H.R. 3713, §6(a)(1); proposed 18 U.S.C. 924(a)(2).

[62] 18 U.S.C. 922(a)(6).

[63] 18 U.S.C. 922(d), (g). A disqualified individual is one who (1) has been convicted of a felony; (2) is a fugitive from justice; (3) is an unlawful user or addicted to a controlled substance; (4) has been adjudicated a mental defective; (5) is an illegal alien; (6) was dishonorably discharged from the Armed Forces; (7) has renounced his U.S. citizenship; (8) is the subject of certain domestic violence restraining orders; or (9) has been convicted of a domestic violence misdemeanor, id.

[64] 18 U.S.C. 922(h).

[65] 18 U.S.C. 922(i).

[66] 18 U.S.C. 922(j).

[67] 18 U.S.C. 922(o).

[68] P.L. 91-513, §§401, 1010; 84 Stat. 1260, 1290 (1970); 21 U.S.C. 841, 960 (1970 ed.).

[69] P.L. 99-570, §§1002, 1004; 100 Stat. 3707-2, 3207-6 (1986); 21 U.S.C. 841, 960 (1988 ed.).

[70] P.L. 111-220, §2; 124 Stat. 2372 (2010); 21 U.S.C. 841, 960.

[71] 18 U.S.C. 3582(c); U.S.S.G. §1B1.10; U.S.S.G. App. C, Amends. 750, 759 (eff. Nov. 1, 2012).

[72] Dorsey v. United States, 132 S. Ct. 2321, 2326 (2012).

[73] 18 U.S.C. 3582)(c)(2).

[74] United States v. Santos-Rivera, 726 F.3d 17, 28 (1st Cir. 2013)(internal citations omitted)("[I]n United States v. Goncalves, we joined ten other Circuit Courts of Appeal in concluding that the FSA is not retroactive for the benefit of a defendant like Carrasquillo-Oscasio, whose

criminal conduct and sentencing occurred before the FSA became law"); see also, United States v. Hodge, 721 F.3d 1279, 1281 (10th Cir. 2013).

[75] United States v. Swangin, 726 F.3d 205, 208 (D.C.Cir. 2013)("Finally, we note that every circuit that has addressed the question post-Dorsey has likewise concluded that courts cannot retroactively apply the Fair Sentencing Act's new mandatory minimums in §3582(c)(2) proceedings to defendants who were sentenced before the Act's effective date"); United States v. Hodge, 721 F.3d at 1281 ("As an initial matter, the FSA does not provide an independent basis for a sentence reduction; only the statutory exceptions in 18 U.S.C. §3882 provide such grounds. In a §3882 proceeding, the court applies the statutory penalties in effect at the time of the original sentencing").

[76] United States v. Reeves, 717 F.3d 647, 650 (8th Cir. 2013)("[E]ight of the nine federal circuits to address the issue have held that the statutory provisions applicable when the defendant was originally sentenced – not the statutory provisions in the Fair Sentencing Act – apply in section 3582(c)(2) proceedings"). The single contrary option was later vacated for en banc rehearing, United States v. Blewett, 719 F.3d 482 (6th Cir. 2013). The divided Blewett panel held that defendants sentenced prior the Fair Sentencing Act's enactment were entitled to its reductions as a matter of equal protection, United States v. Blewett, 719 F.3d at 494.

[77] S. 2123, §106(c); H.R. 3713, §7(c). The section, with changes found only in H.R. 3713 appearing in italics and changes found only in S. 2123 underlined, would read: "No court shall entertain a motion made under this section to reduce a sentence if the sentence was previously imposed or previously reduced to a sentence greater than the applicable mandatory minimum in accordance with the amendments made by sections 2 and 3 of the Fair Sentencing Act of 2010)(Public Law 111-120; 124 Stat. 2372), or if a previous motion made pursuant to sections 2 or 3 of the Sentencing Act or under this section to reduce the sentence was, after the date of enactment of the Act, denied after a complete review of the motion on the merits denied by a court because a reduction in the defendant's term of imprisonment would pose a danger to any person or the community or was denied by a court because of the defendant's post-sentencing conduct. Nothing in this section shall require a court to reduce any sentence pursuant to this section."

[78] H.R. 2944, §404(a)("A court that imposed a sentence for a covered offense, may, on motion of the defendant, the Director of the Bureau of Prisons, the attorney for the Government, or the court, impose a reduced sentence as if sections 2 and 3 of the Fair Sentencing Act of 2010 were in effect as the time the covered offense was committed").

[79] S. 2123, §107, proposed 18 U.S.C. 2261(b)(1).

[80] S. 2123, §107, proposed 18 U.S.C. 2261(b)(2), (3).

[81] 50 U.S.C. 1705.

[82] S. 2123, §108(2), proposed 50 U.S.C. 1705(d)(1), (2)(C), (3)(B), (3)(C). Section 47 of the Arms Export Control Act, 22 U.S.C. 2794(3), (4), defines the term "defense article" to include things like weapons and materials and facilities used to produce and market weapons. The countries subject to embargo are Iraq, North Korea, and the other countries listed in 22 C.F.R. §126.1.

[83] S. 2123, §108(2), proposed 50 U.S.C. 1705(d)(1), (2)(B), (3)(E). "Weapons of mass destruction" includes biological, chemical, and nuclear weapons, as well as explosives, 18 U.S.C. 2332a(c)(2).

[84] S. 2123, §108(2), proposed 50 U.S.C. 1705(d)(1), (2)(A), (3)(A), (3)(D). The entities covered consist of (1) state sponsors of terrorism, as defined in §6(j)(1)(A) of the Export Administration Act of 1979, 50 U.S.C. App. 2405(j)(1)(A); (2) foreign terrorist

organizations as designated under §219(a) of the Immigration and Nationality Act, 8 U.S.C. 1189(a); and (3) persons of Office of Foreign Assets Control's list of designated nationals and blocked persons.

[85] S. 2123, §109(b).

[86] S. 2123, §109(c).

[87] S. 2123, §109(d).

[88] H.R. 2944 §101(a).

[89] H.R. 2944 §101(b).

[90] H.R. 2944 §102(a).

In: Risk Assessment and Sentencing … ISBN: 978-1-63484-561-8
Editor: Julia Campbell

Chapter 3

MANDATORY MINIMUM SENTENCING LEGISLATION IN THE 114TH CONGRESS*

Charles Doyle

SUMMARY

A surprising number of federal crimes carry mandatory minimum terms of imprisonment; that is, they are punishably by imprisonment for a term of not less than some number of years. During the 114th Congress, Members have introduced a number of related proposals. Some would expand the scope of existing mandatory minimum sentencing provisions; others would contract their reach.

The most sweeping proposal is that of Representative Scott (VA) (H.R. 706) and Senator Paul (S. 353), which impacts mandatory minimum sentencing across the board, allowing federal courts to disregard statutory mandatory minimum sentencing requirements in order to avoid conflicts with general sentencing standards.

Other proposals are more narrowly drawn, and speak to a particular class of crime. Representative Polis (H.R. 1013), for example, has suggested decriminalizing marijuana, thereby eliminating the mandatory minimum sentencing provisions now associated with marijuana.

Several bills, including those offered by Senators Cornyn (S. 178), Feinstein (S. 140), and Kirk (S. 572), as well as those offered by

---

* This is an edited, reformatted and augmented version of a Congressional Research Service publication R44006, prepared for Members and Committees of Congress, dated April 29, 2015.

Representatives Poe (H.R. 181, H.R. 296), Granger (H.R. 1201), and Wagner (H.R. 285), would clarify or expand the coverage of a number of federal sex trafficking offenses, in one way or another, thereby increasing the number of defendants facing mandatory minimum sentences.

While proposals relating to sex trafficking would largely increase the number of mandatory minimum sentences imposed, most of the proposals relating to drug trafficking would have the opposite impact. Senator Lee's S. 502 and Representative Labrador's H.R. 920, for instance, would reduce the mandatory minimum sentences that accompany a number of drug trafficking offenses. The same bills would expand the so-called safety valve which allows a court to sentence certain low-level drug offenders below the otherwise applicable mandatory minimum sentence. Finally, Representative Scott's H.R. 1255 would eliminate the distinction between powder and crack cocaine, and as a consequence potentially reduce the number of defendants subject to the more severe drug trafficking mandatory minimums.

Firearms legislation is more varied. Existing law imposes a series of mandatory minimum sentences when a firearm is associated with the commission of a crime of violence or drug trafficking (18 U.S.C. 924(c)). Representative Scott's H.R. 1254 would convert all of Section 924(c)'s mandatory minimums (not-less-than) to statutory maximums (not-more-than). Senator McCain's S. 847 and Representative McSally's H.R. 1588, on the other hand, would make Section 924(c)'s mandatory minimums available not only in cases involving crimes of violence or drug trafficking, but also those involving the smuggling of aliens.

INTRODUCTION

Federal crimes are usually punishable by a statutory maximum term of imprisonment—for example, "imprisoned for not more than 5 years."[1] A surprising number also have statutory minimum terms of imprisonment—for example, "imprisonment which may not be less than 10 years or for life."[2] Under some circumstances, mandatory minimums have proven controversial.[3] Opponents contend that in some instances they can be arbitrary and unduly severe. Proponents contend that they ensure the offenders of the most serious offenses will receive at least some minimum punishment. Legislative proposals in the 114th Congress reflect both perspectives.[4]

A GENERAL EXCEPTION

Federal courts are required to weigh the standards listed in 18 U.S.C. 3553(a) before sentencing a defendant. The standards include things like "the need for the sentence imposed ... to provide just punishment for the offense" and "the need to avoid unwarranted sentence disparities ..."[5] In doing so, however, the courts may not disregard any applicable statutory mandatory minimums.

S. 353 (Senator Paul) and H.R. 706 (Representative Scott (VA)) would permit federal courts to impose a sentence below an otherwise applicable mandatory minimum when necessary to avoid violating the sentencing standards found in Section 3553(a).[6] When exercising the authority, the court would have to provide the government and the defendant a chance to be heard, and to provide a written statement of the Section 3553(a) factors that justify the decision to sentence below the mandatory minimum.[7]

DRUG OFFENSES

The Controlled Substances Act and the Controlled Substances Import and Export Act establish a series of mandatory minimum sentences for violation of their prohibitions. Trafficking—that is, importing, exporting, manufacturing, growing, or possessing with the intent to distribute—a very substantial amount of various highly addictive substances such as more than a kilogram of heroin is punishable by imprisonment for not less than 10 years or more than life.[8] A subsequent conviction carries a sentence of imprisonment for not less than 20 years or more than life.[9] When substantial but lesser amounts are involved, such as100 grams of heroin, sentences of imprisonment for not less than five years or more than life are called for, and imprisonment for not less than 10 years or more than life in the case of a subsequent conviction.[10]

As noted in *Table 1* below, S. 502 (Senator Lee) and H.R. 920 (Representative Labrador) would reduce the mandatory minimum sentences for drug traffickers engaged in manufacture, cultivation, or distribution.[11] They would not reduce the mandatory minimum sentences for traffickers engaged in importing or exporting, other than those who were simply acting as couriers (mules).[12] This is a departure from the proposals in the 113th Congress, which would have reduced the mandatory minimum sentences for traffickers generally, without regard to whether they manufacture or import/export.[13]

Table 1. Terms of Imprisonment: Controlled Substances

Offense	Present Law	S. 502/H.R. 920 (114th Cong.)	S. 1410/H.R. 3382 (113th Cong.)
I. (a)(i) Trafficking: §841(b)(1)(A) substances (e.g., 1 kilo. + of heroin)	not less than 10 years or more than life	not less than 5 years or more than life	not less than 5 years or more than life
(ii) if death or serious injury results (b)(i) one prior violation	not less than 20 years or more than life not less than 20 years or more than life	no change not less than 10 years or more than life	no change not less than 10 years or more than life
(ii) and death or serious injury results	life	no change	no change
(c) two or more prior violations	life	not less than 25 years	no change
II. (a)(i) Trafficking: §841(b)(1)(B) substances (e.g., 100g + of heroin)	not less than 5 years or more than 40 years	not less than 2 years or more than 40 years	not less than 2 years or more than 40 years
(ii) if death or serious injury results	not less than 20 years or more than life	no change	no change
(b)(i)one prior violation	not less than 10 years or more than life	not less than 5 years or more than life	not less than 5 years or more than life
(ii) and death or serious injury results	life	no change	no change
III. (a)(i) Import/export: §960(b)(1) substances (e.g., 1 kilo + of heroin)	not less than 10 years or more than life	no change except for a courier; for a courier, not less than 5 years or more than life	not less than 5 years or more than life

Offense	Present Law	S. 502/H.R. 920 (114th Cong.)	S. 1410/H.R. 3382 (113th Cong.)
(ii) second offense	not less than 20 years or more than life	no change, except for a courier; for a courier, not less than 10 years or more than life	not less than 10 years or more than life
(b)(i) Import/export; §960(b)(2) substances (e.g., 100g + of heroin)	not less than 5 years or more than 40 years	no change, except for couriers; for couriers, not less than 2 years or more than 40 years	not less than 2 years or more than 40 years
(ii) second offense	not less than10 years or more than life	no change, except for couriers; for couriers, not less than 5 years or more than life	not less than 5 years or more than life

Source: Congressional Research Service, based on S. 502/H.R. 920 (114th Cong.); S. 1410/H.R. 3382 (113th Cong.); and 21 U.S.C. 841, 960.

Safety Valve

The so-called safety valve provision of 18 U.S.C. 3553(f) allows a court to sentence qualified defendants below the statutory mandatory minimum in controlled substance trafficking and possession cases.[14] To qualify, a defendant may not have used violence in the course of the offense.[15] He must not have played a managerial role in the offense if it involved group participation.[16] The offense must not have resulted in a death or serious bodily injury.[17] The defendant must make full disclosure of his involvement in the offense, providing the government with all the information and evidence at his disposal.[18] Finally, the defendant must have a virtually spotless criminal record, that is, not more than 1 criminal history point.[19]

Criminal history points and categories are a feature of the U.S. Sentencing Commission's Sentencing Guidelines. The Guidelines assign points based on the sentences imposed for prior state and federal convictions. For example, the Guidelines assign 1 point for any past conviction that resulted in a sentence of less than incarceration for 60 days; 2 points for any conviction resulting in a sentence of incarceration for at least 60 days; and 3 points for any conviction resulting in a sentence of incarceration of more than a year and a month.[20] Criminal History Category I consists of zero or 1 point, Criminal History Category II of 2 or 3 points.[21]

The Sentencing Commission's report on mandatory minimum sentences suggested that Congress consider expanding safety valve eligibility to defendants with 2 or possibly 3 criminal history points.[22] The report indicated that under the Guidelines a defendant's criminal record "can have a disproportionate and excessively severe cumulative sentencing impact on certain drug offenders."[23] It explained that the Guidelines are construed to ensure that the sentence they recommend in a given case calls for a term of imprisonment that is not less than an applicable mandatory minimum.[24] In addition, the drug offenses have escalated mandatory minimums for repeat offenders.[25] Moreover, similarly situated drug offenders may be treated differently, because states punish simple drug possession differently and prosecutors decide when to press recidivism qualifications differently.[26]

The Lee and Labrador bills (S. 502/H.R. 920) would expand safety valve eligibility from defendants with no more than 1 criminal history point to those with no more than 3 points.[27] S. 1410, as voted out of the Senate Judiciary Committee during the last Congress, would have expanded safety valve eligibility from defendants with no more than 1 criminal history point to those with no more than 2 points, if they avoided certain disqualifications.[28] A defendant would have been ineligible for the expanded 2-point criminal history safety valve threshold if he had a prior conviction for a federal firearms offense,[29] sex offense,[30] crime of terrorism,[31] RICO predicate offense,[32] or conspiracy to use or invest drug profits.[33] The current proposals have no such limitation.

Cocaine Sentencing

Originally, the Controlled Substances Act made no distinction between powder cocaine and crack cocaine (cocaine base).[34] The 1986 Anti-Drug Abuse Act introduced a 100-1 sentencing ratio between the two, so that trafficking in 50 grams of crack cocaine carried the same penalties as trafficking in 5,000 grams of powder cocaine.[35] The 2010 Fair Sentencing Act replaced it with the present 500-28 ratio, so that trafficking in 280 grams of crack cocaine carries the same penalties as 5,000 grams of powder cocaine.[36] It also abolished the mandatory minimum for simple crack cocaine possession that the 1988 Anti-Drug Abuse Act had established.[37] The Sentencing Commission subsequently revised the Sentencing Guidelines to reflect the change, and made the modification retroactively applicable at the discretion of the sentencing court.[38]

H.R. 1255 (Representative Scott (VA)) would eliminate the sentencing distinction between powder and crack cocaine by eliminating the cocaine base specific references.[39] Trafficking in cocaine would carry the same penalties regardless of whether the substance was powder or crack cocaine.[40]

Fair Sentencing Retroactivity

The Fair Sentencing Act reductions apply to cocaine offenses committed thereafter. They also apply to offenses committed beforehand when sentencing occurs after the time of enactment.[41] Federal courts have discretion to reduce a sentence imposed under a Sentencing Guideline that was subsequently substantially reduced.[42] The Fair Sentencing Act (FSA), however, does not apply to sentences imposed prior to its enactment,[43] and it does not apply in sentence reduction hearings triggered by new Sentencing Guidelines.[44] In such proceedings, the courts remain bound by the mandatory minimums in effect prior to enactment of the FSA.[45]

S. 502 (Senator Lee) and H.R. 920 (Representative Labrador) would allow a court to reduce a previously imposed sentence for crack cocaine possession or trafficking, consistent with the FSA, on its own or at the behest of the defendant, prosecutor, or Bureau of Prisons.[46] They would also permit a court to reduce such sentences, but would have limited the authority to instances in which the defendant had not been previously granted or denied a similar reduction.[47] The Judiciary Committee's version of S. 1410 (113th Cong.) contained identical provisions.[48]

Sentencing Guideline Reconciliation

S. 502 and H.R. 920 would direct the United States Sentencing Commission to review and propose amendments to the federal Sentencing Guidelines in order to reflect the changes the bills call for and the changes the FSA introduced.[49]

The Sentencing Reform Act created the Sentencing Commission and authorizes it to propose Sentencing Guidelines.[50] It also authorizes the Commission to periodically review and propose amendments to the

Guidelines.[51] Once considered binding, the Guidelines still substantially limit the sentences a federal court may impose.[52] A court must correctly calculate the Guidelines' recommended sentencing range, and it must justify any deviation.[53]

The bills would instruct the Commission to conduct this reexamination with six factors in mind:

- the need to minimize the risk that the federal prison population would exceed the system's capacity;
- the findings and recommendations of the Commission's report on mandatory minimum sentences;
- the fiscal implications of any changes to the Guidelines;
- relevant public safety concerns;
- congressional intent to maintain appropriately severe penalties for violent, repeat, and serious drug traffickers; and
- the need to reduce and prevent racial sentencing disparities.[54]

Marijuana Sentencing

The Controlled Substances Act prohibits cultivation, distribution, possession with intent to distribute, and simple possession of marijuana.[55] Those prohibitions carry with them mandatory minimum sentences when substantial amounts of marijuana are involved. Thus, cultivation, distribution, or possession with intent to distribute "1,000 kilograms [2,204.6 lbs.] or more of a mixture or substance containing a detectable amount of marihuana, or 1,000 or more marihuana plants regardless of weight" is punishable by

> [A] term of imprisonment which may not be less than 10 years or more than life and if death or serious bodily injury results from the use of such substance shall be not less than 20 years or more than life ... If any person commits such a violation after a prior conviction for a felony drug offense has become final, such person shall be sentenced to a term of imprisonment which may not be less than 20 years and not more than life imprisonment and if death or serious bodily injury results from the use of such substance shall be sentenced to life imprisonment ... If any person commits a violation of this subparagraph ... after two or more prior convictions for a felony drug offense have become final, such person

> shall be sentenced to a mandatory term of life imprisonment without release and fined in accordance with the preceding sentence.[56]

If the offense instead involves a lesser amount, that is, less than 1,000 kilograms, but "100 kilograms (220.46 lbs.) or more of a mixture or substance containing a detectable amount of marihuana, or 100 or more marihuana plants regardless of weight," the offense is punishable by

> [A] term of imprisonment which may not be less than 5 years and not more than 40 years and if death or serious bodily injury results from the use of such substance shall be not less than 20 years or more than life ... If any person commits such a violation after a prior conviction for a felony drug offense has become final, such person shall be sentenced to a term of imprisonment which may not be less than 10 years and not more than life imprisonment and if death or serious bodily injury results from the use of such substance shall be sentenced to life imprisonment....[57]

H.R. 1013 (Representative Polis) would eliminate mandatory minimum sentences for trafficking in marijuana by removing marijuana from the coverage of the Controlled Substances Act.[58]

ATTORNEY GENERAL REPORTS

S. 502 (Senator Lee) and H.R. 920 (Representative Labrador) would also direct the Attorney General to prepare two reports covering federal criminal statutes, generally both those that feature mandatory sentencing provisions and those that do not. The first would address the impact of the bill's provisions, including an indication of how the savings realized from the reduction in mandatory minimum sentences would be used to reduce prison overcrowding and to contribute to crime prevention.[59]

The second would provide an inventory of federal criminal statutory and regulatory offenses.[60] The report would be required to indicate the range of penalties that accompany each offense, the mens rea element for each offense, and the regularity with which each offense has been prosecuted.[61] For the regulatory offenses, inventory and related information would have to be broken down on an agency-by-agency basis.[62]

The same provisions appeared in S. 1410 as it was taken to the floor during the 113th Congress.[63]

FIREARMS

Section 924(c), in its current form, imposes one of several different minimum sentences when a firearm is used or possessed in furtherance of another federal crime of violence or drug trafficking.[64] The mandatory minimums, imposed in addition to the sentence imposed for the underlying crime of violence or drug trafficking, vary, depending upon the circumstances:

- imprisonment for not less than five years, unless one of the higher mandatory minimums below applies;
- imprisonment for not less than seven years, if a firearm is brandished;
- imprisonment for not less than 10 years, if a firearm is discharged;
- imprisonment for not less than 10 years, if a firearm is a short-barreled rifle or shotgun or is a semi-automatic weapon;
- imprisonment for not less than 15 years, if the offense involves armor-piercing ammunition;
- imprisonment for not less than 25 years, if the offender has a prior conviction for violation of Section 924(c);
- imprisonment for not less than 30 years, if the firearm is a machine gun or destructive device or is equipped with a silencer;[65] and
- imprisonment for life, if the offender has a prior conviction for violation of Section 924(c) and if the firearm is a machine gun or destructive device or is equipped with a silencer.[66]

H.R. 1254 (Representative Scott (VA)) would convert all of Section 924(c)'s mandatory minimum penalties to maximum penalties. Each of its not-less-than penalties would become notmore-than penalties.[67] So, for example, possession of a shotgun in furtherance of a crime of violence or of drug trafficking would be punishable by imprisonment for not more than 10 years. Possession of a machine gun in furtherance of such an offense would be punishable by imprisonment for not more than 30 years.

The Scott bill would append in large measure the procedure used in Controlled Substance Act cases to establish the existence of a qualifying prior conviction, 21 U.S.C. 851.[68] It would, however, drop the provision in Section 851 that affords the defendant the right to have the question presented to the grand jury in the case of serious enhancements.[69] It would also abandon the provision that bars questioning the validity of remote convictions.[70] H.R. 1254 is a twin of a proposal offered by Representative Scott in the 113th Congress.[71]

S. 847 (Senator McCain) and H.R. 1588 (Representative McSally), in contrast, would enlarge the coverage of Section 924(c) by adding alien smuggling, 8 U.S.C. 1324(a), 1327, or 1328, to violent crimes and drug trafficking as predicate offenses which trigger Section 924(c)'s mandatory minimum sentences.[72] Thus, for example, a defendant, in possession of a firearm in furtherance of alien smuggling, would be subject to imprisonment for not less than five years. The proposal has a number of antecedents in the 113th Congress.[73]

SEX OFFENSES

The Mann Act (travel or transportation for unlawful sexual purposes) and 18 U.S.C. 1591 (commercial sex trafficking) contain several provisions which outlaw sexual misconduct punishable by mandatory minimum sentences. A number of proposals would either clarify or expand the reach of those provisions.

Commercial Sex Trafficking

Liability of Patrons

Section 1591 outlaws commercial sex trafficking. More precisely, it outlaws

- knowingly
- recruiting, enticing, harboring, transporting, providing, obtaining, or maintaining another individual
- knowing or with reckless disregard of the fact that
    - the individual will be used to engage commercial sexual activity
- either as a child or by virtue of the use of fraud or coercion
- when the activity occurs in or affects interstate or foreign commerce, or occurs within the special maritime or territorial jurisdiction of the United States.[74]

It outlaws separately profiting from such a venture.[75]

Offenders face the prospect of life imprisonment with a mandatory minimum term of not less than 15 years (not less than 10 years if the victim is between the ages of 14 and 18).[76] The same penalties apply to anyone who attempts to violate the provisions of Section 1591.[77]

There have been suggestions to expand Section 1591 to cover advertisers and to more explicitly cover the customers of a commercial sex trafficking scheme. At first glance, Section 1591 does not appear to cover the customers of a sex trafficking enterprise. Moreover, in the absence of a specific provision, mere customers ordinarily are not considered either co-conspirators or accessories before the fact in a prostitution ring.[78] Nevertheless, the United States Court of Appeals found that the language of Section 1591(a) applied to the case of two customers caught in a law enforcement "sting" who attempted to purchase the services of what they believed were child prostitutes.[79] "The ordinary and natural meaning of 'obtains' and the other terms Congress selected in drafting §1591 are broad enough to encompass the actions of both suppliers and purchasers of commercial sex acts," the court declared.[80]

S. 178, H.R. 181, and a number of other bills would explicitly confirm this construction by amending Section 1591(a) to read in part "Whoever knowingly ... recruits, entices, harbors, transports, provides, obtains, maintains, or *patronizes, or solicits* by any means any person ..." (language of the proposed amendment in italics).[81]

Age: Prosecutors' Burden

The same bills often amend the "knowledge of age" element in Section 1591(c) to reflect its clarifying amendment with respect to the customers of a commercial sex trafficking venture. The law now absolves the government of the obligation to prove that the defendant knew the victim was a child, if it can show that the defendant had an opportunity to "observe" the victim.[82] The proposal would make it clear that the government would be equally absolved regardless of whether the defendant were a consumer or purveyor of a child's sexual commercial services, as long as it establishes that the defendant had an opportunity to observe the child: "In a prosecution under subsection (a)(1) in which the defendant had a reasonable opportunity to observe the person so recruited, enticed, harbored, transported, provided, obtained, maintained, *patronized, or solicited* the Government need not prove that the defendant knew, *or recklessly disregarded the fact*, that the person had not attained the age of 18 years," 18 U.S.C. 1591(c) (language of the proposed amendment in italics).[83]

Advertisers

Proposals to explicitly cover advertisers might also be seen as a matter of simply sharpening existing law. Anyone who aids and abets the commission of a federal crime by another merits the same punishment as the individual who actually commits the crime.[84] Liability for aiding and abetting requires that a defendant embrace the crime of another and consciously do something to contribute to its success.[85]

One of Section 1591's distinctive features is that its action elements—recruiting, harboring, transporting, providing, obtaining—are activities that might be associated with aiding and abetting the operation of a prostitution enterprise. Section 1591, read literally, does not outlaw operating a prostitution business; it outlaws the steps leading up to or associated with operating a prostitution business—recruiting, harboring, transporting, etc. Strictly construed, advertising in aid of recruitment, harboring, transporting, or one of the other action elements might qualify as aiding and abetting a violation of Section 1591; advertising the availability of a prostitute might not.

Yet one court suggests that Section 1591 does outlaw operating a prostitution business, at least for purposes of aiding and abetting liability, and that by implication advertising might constitute aiding and abetting a violation of the section:

> Pringler first argues that the evidence is insufficient to support his conviction for aiding and abetting the sex trafficking of a minor [in violation of Section 1591].... We disagree. The record is not devoid of evidence to support the jury's verdict and show Pringler's integral role in the criminal venture. Pringler took the money that Norman and B.L. earned from their prostitution and used some of it to pay for hotel rooms where the women met their patrons. Pringler bought the laptop Norman and B.L. used to advertise their services. He drove Norman and B.L. to "outcall" appointments, and he took photographs of Norman, which he had planned for use in advertisements.[86]

Some bills, H.R. 285 and S. 572, for example, would amend Section 1591(a)(1) to outlaw knowingly advertising a person, knowing the victim would be used for prostitution.[87] Proponents might suggest that "advertising" would seem to fit snugly within the litany of Section 1591's action elements.

Section 1591 now requires the government to prove either that the defendant knew of the victim's underage or coerced status or recklessly disregarded it. The proposal would expose the trafficker and the profiteer to liability based on different levels of knowledge. The liability for advertising traffickers would require that they knew of or recklessly disregarded the victim's status. The liability for advertising profiteers would require that they knew of the victim's status.[88]

Knowledge is obviously a more demanding standard than reckless disregard, but the dividing line between the two is not always easily discerned, in part because of the doctrine of willful blindness. The doctrine describes the circumstances under which a jury may be instructed by the court that it may infer knowledge on the part of a defendant. Worded variously, the doctrine applies where evidence indicates that the defendant sought to avoid the guilty knowledge.[89]

Since the element is worded in the alternative—knowing or in reckless disregard of the fact—the courts have rarely distinguished the two. One interpretation comes from comparable wording in an immigration offense which outlaws transporting an alien knowing or acting in reckless disregard of the fact that the alien is in this country illegally: "To act with reckless disregard of the fact means to be aware of but consciously and carelessly ignore facts and circumstances clearly indicating that the person transported was an alien who had entered or remained in the United States illegally."[90] The courts refer to a similar unreasonable indifference standard when speaking of the veracity required for the issuance of a warrant.[91]

Mann Act

The Mann Act criminalizes, among other things, (1) interstate or foreign transportation of a child for purposes of prostitution or other unlawful sexual purposes; (2) interstate or foreign travel for purposes of engaging in "illicit sexual activity" with a child; and (3) overseas travel of U.S. nationals followed by illicit sexual activities with a child.[92]

Defendants enjoy an affirmative defense in "illicit sexual activity" cases, if they can establish by a preponderance of the evidence that they reasonably believed that the victim was over 18 years of age.[93]

S. 178, H.R. 181, and other bills would limit the defense to cases where the defendant establishes the reasonableness of his belief by clear and convincing evidence.[94] The difference between preponderance of the evidence and clear and convincing is the difference between more likely than not[95] and highly probable.[96] Many of these same proposals would amend the "illicit sexual activity" definition to include child pornography cases,[97] with the result that interstate or foreign travel associated with the production of child pornography would be clear violations of the Mann Act's Section 2423(b)(interstate or foreign travel for purposes of such production), Section 2423(c)(foreign travel followed by such production), and Section 2423(d)(commercially facilitating such travel), each of which is punishable by imprisonment for not more than 30 years.[98]

End Notes

[1] 18 U.S.C. 1001(a)(relating to false statements); see also 18 U.S.C. 1955(a)(relating to operating an illegal gambling business); 18 U.S.C. 2339B("imprisoned not more than 15 years")(relating to providing material support to designated terrorist organizations); 18 U.S.C. 1341("imprison not more than 20 years")(relating to mail fraud).

[2] See, generally, CRS Report RL32040, Federal Mandatory Minimum Sentencing Statutes.

[3] See, generally, United States Sentencing Commission, Report to the Congress: Mandatory Minimum Penalties in the Federal Criminal Justice System, Policy Views About Mandatory Minimum Penalties, 85-103 (October 2011), available at http://www.ussc.gov/Legislative_and_Public_Affairs/Congressional_Testimony_and_Reports/Mandatory_Minimum-Penalties/20111031_Rtc_Mandatory_Minimum.cfm.

[4] Many of the proposals had antecedents in the 113th Congress, as discussed in CRS Report R43296, Mandatory Minimum Sentencing Legislation in the 113th Congress, by Charles Doyle, from which this report has borrowed heavily. Portions of the analysis here are also reflected in another CRS report by the same author, CRS Report R44007, Sex Trafficking: Proposals in the 114th Congress to Amend Federal Criminal Law.

[5] 18 U.S.C. 3553(a)("The court shall impose a sentence sufficient, but not greater than necessary, to comply with the purposes set forth in paragraph (2) of this subsection. The court, in determining the particular sentence to be imposed, shall consider- (1) the nature and circumstances of the offense and the history and characteristics of the defendant; (2) the need for the sentence imposed- (A) to reflect the seriousness of the offense, to promote respect for the law, and to provide just punishment for the offense; (B) to afford adequate deterrence to criminal conduct; (C) to protect the public from further crimes of the defendant; and (D) to provide the defendant with needed educational or vocational training, medical care, or other correctional treatment in the most effective manner; (3) the kinds of sentences available; (4) the kinds of sentence and the sentencing range established ... issued by the Sentencing Commission ... (5) any pertinent policy statement ... issued by the Sentencing Commission ... (6) the need to avoid unwarranted sentence disparities among defendants with similar records who have been found guilty of similar conduct; and (7) the need to provide restitution to any victims of the offense").

[6] H.R. 706, §2, proposed 18 U.S.C. 3553(g)(1); S. 353, §2, proposed 18 U.S.C. 3553(g)(1). Senator Paul and Representative Scott introduced identical legislation in the 113th Congress, S. 619 (113th Cong.) and H.R. 1695 (113th Cong.)

[7] H.R. 706, §2, proposed 18 U.S.C. 3553(g)(2), (3); S. 353, §2, proposed 18 U.S.C. 3553(g)(2), (3).

[8] 21 U.S.C. 841(b)(1)(A); 21 U.S.C. 960(b)(1). The threshold amounts covered by the sections in addition to a kilogram of heroin are "(ii) 5 kilograms or more of a mixture or substance containing a detectable amount of- (I) coca leaves, except coca leaves and extracts of coca leaves from which cocaine, ecgonine, and derivatives of ecgonine or their salts have been removed; (II) cocaine, its salts, optical and geometric isomers, and salts of isomers; (III) ecgonine, its derivatives, their salts, isomers, and salts of isomers; or (IV) any compound, mixture, or preparation which contains any quantity of any of the substances referred to in subclauses (I) through (III); (iii) 280 grams or more of a mixture or substance described in clause (ii) which contains cocaine base; (iv) 100 grams or more of phencyclidine (PCP) or 1 kilogram or more of a mixture or substance containing a detectable amount of phencyclidine (PCP); (v) 10 grams or more of a mixture or substance containing a detectable amount of lysergic acid diethylamide (LSD); (vi) 400 grams or more of a mixture or substance containing a detectable amount of N-phenyl-N- [1- (2-phenylethyl) -4-piperidinyl] propanamide or 100 grams or more of a mixture or substance containing a detectable amount of any analogue of Nphenyl-N-[1-(2-phenylethyl)-4-piperidinyl] propanamide; (vii) 1,000 kilograms or more of a mixture or substance containing a detectable amount of marihuana, or 1,000 or more marihuana plants regardless of weight; or (viii) 50 grams or more of methamphetamine, its salts, isomers, and salts of its isomers or 500 grams or more of a mixture or substance containing a detectable amount of methamphetamine, its salts, isomers, or salts of its isomers." 21 U.S.C. 841(b)(1)(ii)-(vii).

[9] 21 U.S.C. 841(b)(1)(A); 21 U.S.C. 960(b)(1)("... If any person commits such a violation after a prior conviction for a felony drug offense has become final, such person shall be sentenced to a term of imprisonment which may not be less than 20 years and not more than life imprisonment.... ").

[10] 21 U.S.C. 841(b)(1)(B); 21 U.S.C. 960(b)(2). Beyond 100 grams of heroin, the threshold amounts for this lower sentencing plateau are "(ii) 500 grams or more of a mixture or substance containing a detectable amount of ... cocaine ... (iii) 28 grams or more of a mixture or substance described in clause (ii) which contains cocaine base; (iv) 10 grams or more of phencyclidine (PCP) ... (v) 1 gram or more of a mixture or substance containing a detectable amount of lysergic acid diethylamide (LSD); (vi) 40 grams or more of a mixture or substance containing a detectable amount of ... propanamide ... (vii) 100 kilograms or more of a mixture or substance containing a detectable amount of marihuana ... or (viii) 5 grams or more of methamphetamine.... " 21 U.S.C. 841(b)(1)(B)(ii)-(vii).

[11] S. 502, §4(a); H.R. 920, §4(a).

[12] S. 502, §4(b); H.R. 920, §4(b).

[13] S. 1410 (113th Cong.), §4; H.R. 3382 (113th Cong.), §4.

[14] 18 U.S.C. 3553(f)("Notwithstanding any other provision of law, in the case of an offense under section 401, 404, or 406 of the Controlled Substances Act (21 U.S.C. 841, 844, 846) or section 1010 or 1013 of the Controlled Substances Import and Export Act (21 U.S.C. 960, 963), the court shall impose a sentence pursuant to guidelines promulgated by the United States Sentencing Commission under section 994 of title 28 without regard to any statutory minimum sentence, if the court finds at sentencing, after the Government has been afforded the opportunity to make a recommendation ...").

[15] 18 U.S.C. 3553(f)(2)("... if the court finds at sentencing ... that ... (2) the defendant did not use violence or credible threats of violence or possess a firearm or other dangerous weapon (or induce another participant to do so) in connection with the offense").

[16] 18 U.S.C. 3553(f)(4)("... if the court finds at sentencing ... that ... (4) the defendant was not an organizer, leader, manager, or supervisor of others in the offense, as determined under the

sentencing guidelines and was not engaged in a continuing criminal enterprise, as defined in section 408 of the Controlled Substances Act").

17 18 U.S.C. 3553(f)(3)("... if the court finds at sentencing ... that ... (3) the offense did not result in death or serious bodily injury to any person").

18 18 U.S.C. 3553(f)(5)("... if the court finds at sentencing ... that ... (5) not later than the time of the sentencing hearing, the defendant has truthfully provided to the Government all information and evidence the defendant has concerning the offense or offenses that were part of the same course of conduct or of a common scheme or plan, but the fact that the defendant has no relevant or useful other information to provide or that the Government is already aware of the information shall not preclude a determination by the court that the defendant has complied with this requirement").

19 18 U.S.C. 3553(f)(1)("... if the court finds at sentencing ... that - (1) the defendant does not have more than 1 criminal history point, as determined under the sentencing guidelines").

20 U.S.S.G. §4A1.1.

21 U.S.S.G. Sentencing Table.

22 United States Sentencing Commission, Report to the Congress: Mandatory Minimum Penalties in the Federal Criminal Justice System, 355 (October 2011).

23 Id. at 352.

24 Id.

25 Id.

26 Id. at 353 ("Interviews of prosecutors and defense attorneys in 13 districts confirm that different districts have adopted different practices with respect to filing the necessary information required to seek an enhanced penalty under 21 U.S.C. §851 [relating to proof of a prior conviction] in part because of its severity. The structure of the recidivist provisions in 21 U.S.C. §§841 and 960 fosters inconsistent application, in part, because their applicability turns on the varying statutory maximum penalties for state drug offenses").

27 S. 502//H.R. 920, §2, proposed 18 U.S.C. 3553(f)(1). The bill sets the ceiling at criminal history category II, that is, not more than 3 criminal history points, U.S.S.G. ch.5, pt. A.

28 S. 1410 (113th Cong.), §2, proposed 18 U.S.C. 3553(f)(1)(B).

29 As proscribed under 18 U.S.C. 922, 924.

30 As defined under §111 of the Adam Walsh Child Protection and Safety Act of 2006 (42 U.S.C. 16911).

31 As defined in 18 U.S.C. 2332b(g)(5).

32 As identified in 18 U.S.C. 1961(1).

33 As proscribed under 18 U.S.C 371 and 21 U.S.C. 854.

34 P.L. 91-513, §§401, 1010; 84 Stat. 1260, 1290 (1970); 21 U.S.C. 841, 960 (1970 ed.).

35 P.L. 99-570, §§1002, 1004; 100 Stat. 3207-2, 3207-6; 21 U.S.C. 841, 960 (1988 ed.).

36 P.L. 111-220, §2, 124 Stat. 2372, 21 U.S.C. 841, 960.

37 P.L. 111-220, §3, 124 Stat. 2372, 21 U.S.C. 844.

38 18 U.S.C. 3582(c); U.S.S.G. 1B1.10; U.S.S.G. App. C, Amends. 750, 759.

39 H.R. 1255, §2, proposed 21 U.S.C. 841(b)(1)(A), 841(b)(1)(B), 960(b)(1), 960(b)(2). Representative Scott introduced a comparable bill in the last Congress, H.R. 2372 (113th Cong.).

40 Id.

41 Dorsey v. United States, 132 S.Ct. 2321, 2326 (2012).

42 18 U.S.C. 3582(c)(2).

43 United States v. Santos-Rivera, 726 F3.d 17, 28 (1st Cir. 2013)(internal citations omitted)("[I]n United States v. Goncalves, we joined ten of our fellow Circuit Courts of Appeal in

concluding that the FSA is not retroactive for the benefit of a defendant like Carrasquillo-Ocasio, whose criminal conduct and sentencing occurred before the FSA became law"); see also United States v. Hodge, 721 F.3d 1279, 1281 (10th Cir. 2013).

44 United States v. Swangin, 726 F.3d 205, 208 (D.C.Cir. 2013)("Finally, we note that every circuit that has addressed the question post-Dorsey has likewise concluded that courts cannot retroactively apply the Fair Sentencing Act's new mandatory minimums in §3582(c)(2) proceedings to defendants who were sentenced before the Act's effective date"); United States v. Hodge, 721 F.3d at 1281 ("As an initial matter, the FSA does not provide an independent basis for a sentence reduction; only the statutory exceptions in 18 U.S.C.§3582 provide such grounds. In a §3582 proceeding, the court applies the statutory penalties in effect at the time of the original sentencing").

45 United States v. Reeves, 717 F.3d 647, 650 (8th Cir. 2013)("[E]ight of the nine federal circuits to address the issue have held that the statutory provisions applicable when the defendant was originally sentenced—not the statutory provisions in the Fair Sentencing Act—apply in section 3582(c)(2) proceedings"). The single contrary opinion was later vacated for en banc rehearing, United States v. Blewett, 719 F.3d 482 (6th Cir. 2013). The divided Blewett panel held that defendants sentenced prior to the FSA's enactment were entitled to its reductions as a matter of equal protection, United States v. Blewett, 719 F.3d at 494.

46 S. 502 (Sen. Lee), §3; H.R. 920 (Rep. Labrador), §3.

47 S. 502, §3(c); H.R. 920, §3(c).

48 S. 1410 (113th Cong.), §3.

49 S. 502, §5(a); H.R. 920, §5(a). S. 1410, as reported out of the Judiciary Committee in the 113th Congress, had an identical provision, S. 1410 (113th Cong.), §5.

50 28 U.S.C. 991, 994.

51 28 U.S.C. 994(p).

52 18 U.S.C. 3553(b)(1)(purporting to make the Guidelines binding), found unconstitutional but severable in United States v. Booker, 543 U.S. 220 (2005).

53 United States v. Gall, 552 U.S. 38, 49-50(2007)("[A] district court should begin all sentencing proceedings by correctly calculating the applicable Guidelines range.... If he decides that an outside-Guidelines sentence is warranted, he must consider the extent of the deviation and ensure that the justification is sufficiently compelling to support the degree of the variance").

54 S. 502, §5(b); H.R. 920, §5(b).

55 21 U.S.C. 841(a), 844.

56 21 U.S.C. 841(b)(1)(A).

57 21 U.S.C. 841(b)(1)(B).

58 H.R. 1255, §101.

59 S. 502, §6; H.R. 920, §6.

60 S. 502, §7; H.R. 920, §7.

61 S. 502, §7(b), (c); H.R. 920, §7(b), (c).

62 S. 502, §7(c); H.R. 920, §7(c).

63 S. 1410 (113th Cong.), §6 (savings), §7 (inventory).

64 18 U.S.C. 924(c).

65 18 U.S.C. 921(4)("The term 'destructive device' means- (A) any explosive, incendiary, or poison gas- (i) bomb, (ii) grenade, (iii) rocket having a propellant charge of more than four ounces, (iv) missile having an explosive or incendiary charge of more than one-quarter ounce, (v) mine, or (vi) device similar to any of the devices described in the preceding clauses; ...").

[66] 18 U.S.C. 924(c)(1), (5).

[67] H.R. 1254, §2(1), (2), proposed 18 U.S.C. 924(c)(1)(A), (B), (C), (5)(A).

[68] H.R. 1254, §2(3), proposed 18 U.S.C. 924(c)(6).

[69] Id. ("The provisions of ... 21 U.S.C. 851, other than subsections (a)(2) and (e) ... shall apply to sentencing for convictions under this subsection.... "). 21 U.S.C. 851(a)(2) provides "An information may not be filed under this section if the increased punishment which may be imposed is imprisonment for a term in excess of three years unless the person either waived or was afforded prosecution by indictment for the offense for which such increased punishment may be imposed."

[70] Id. ("The provisions of ... 21 U.S.C. 851, other than subsections (a)(2) and (e) ... shall apply to sentencing for convictions under this subsection.... "). 21 U.S.C. 851(e) provides "No person who stands convicted of an offense under this part may challenge the validity of any prior conviction alleged under this section which occurred more than five years before the date of the information alleging such prior conviction."

[71] H.R. 2405 (113th Cong.).

[72] S. 847, §2(b), proposed 18 U.S.C. 924(c)(1), (2); H.R. 1588, §2(b), proposed 18 U.S.C. 924(c)(1), (2).

[73] H.R. 4961 (113th Cong.)(Rep. McCaul), §4(d), proposed 18 U.S.C. 924(c)("prohibiting carrying or use of a firearm during and in relation to an alien smuggling crime[, i.e., felonies punishable under 8 U.S.C. 1324(a), 1327, 1328]"); S. 2561 (113th Cong.)(Sen. McCain), §4(d), proposed 18 U.S.C. 924(c); S. 2619(113th Cong.)(Sen. McCain), §5(a)(2), proposed 18 U.S.C. 924(c); S. 2743, §1204(a)(2), proposed 18 U.S.C. 924(c); S. 2773 (113th Cong.)(Sen. Cornyn), §1204(a)(2), proposed 18 U.S.C. 924(c).

[74] 18 U.S.C. 1591(a): "Whoever knowingly - (1) in or affecting interstate or foreign commerce, or within the special maritime and territorial jurisdiction of the United States, recruits, entices, harbors, transports, provides, obtains, or maintains by any means a person; or (2) benefits, financially or by receiving anything of value, from participation in a venture which has engaged in an act described in violation of paragraph (1), "knowing, or in reckless disregard of the fact, that means of force, threats of force, fraud, coercion described in subsection (e)(2), or any combination of such means will be used to cause the person to engage in a commercial sex act, or that the person has not attained the age of 18 years and will be caused to engage in a commercial sex act, shall be punished as provided in subsection (b)."

[75] 18 U.S.C. 1951(a)(2)(quoted above).

[76] 18 U.S.C. 1591(b).

[77] 18 U.S.C. 1594(a).

[78] See e.g., United States v. Southard, 700 F.2d 1, 20 (1st Cir. 1983)("[O]ne having intercourse with a prostitute is not liable for aiding and abetting prostitution"); see, generally, CRS Report R43769, Aiding, Abetting, and the Like: An Overview of 18 U.S.C. 2, by Charles Doyle.

[79] United States v. Jungers, 702 F.3d 1066 (8th Cir. 2013).

[80] Id. at 1071.

[81] H.R. 181 (Rep. Poe), §6(1), (2), proposed 18 U.S.C. 1591(a); H.R. 296 (Rep. Poe), §9(a)(1), (2), proposed 18 U.S.C. 1591(a); H.R. 1201 (Rep. Granger), §2(a)(1), (2), proposed 18 U.S.C. 1591(a); S. 140 (Sen. Feinstein), §2(a)(1), (2), proposed 18 U.S.C. 1591(a); S. 178 (Sen. Cornyn), §9(a)(1), (2), proposed 18 U.S.C. 1591(a); see also H.Rept. 113- 450, at 15-6 (2014)(discussing a similar proposal in the 113th Congress). Here and hereinafter references

to H.R. 181 and later references to H.R. 285 allude to those measures as passed by the House.

[82] United States v. Robinson, 702 F.3d 22, 26 (2d Cir. 2012)("[T]his provision [Section 1591(c)], when applicable, imposes strict liability with regard to the defendant's awareness of the victim's age, thus relieving the government's usual burden to prove knowledge or reckless disregard of the victim's underage status under §1591(a)").

[83] H.R. 181, §6(3), proposed 18 U.S.C. 1591(c); H.R. 296, §9(a)(3), proposed 18 U.S.C. 1591(c); S. 140, §2(a)(3), proposed 18 U.S.C. 1591(c); S. 178, §9(a)(3), proposed 18 U.S.C. 1591(c); the House report with respect to comparable language in an earlier proposal observed that "[t]his clarification is intended to direct law enforcement's investigative and prosecutorial focus on the purchasers of these illegal services, who create the market for the traffickers," H.Rept. 113-450, at 16 (2014).

[84] 18 U.S.C. 2(a)("Whoever commits an offense against the United States or aids, abets, counsels, commands, induces or procures its commission, is punishable as a principal").

[85] Rosemond v. United States, 134 S.Ct. 1240, 1245 (2014), quoting, Central Bank of Denver, N.A. v. First Interstate Bank of Denver, N.A., 511 U.S. 164, 181 (1994)("[T]hose who provide knowing aid to persons committing federal crimes, with the intent to facilitate the crime, are themselves committing a crime"); see also United States v. Pringler, 765 F.3d 445, 449 (5th Cir. 2014)("To hold a defendant liable for aiding and abetting an offense, the government must show that elements of the substantive offense occurred and that the defendant associated with the criminal activity, participated in it, and acted to help it succeed").

[86] Id. at 449-51.

[87] E.g., H.R. 285, §2(a), proposed 18 U.S.C. 1591(a)(1); S. 572, §2(a), proposed 18 U.S.C. 1591(a)(1).

[88] Should the proposal be enacted 18 U.S.C. 1591(a) would read in pertinent part (proposed language in italics): "Whoever knowingly - (1) in or affecting interstate or foreign commerce, or within the special maritime and territorial jurisdiction of the United States, recruits ... advertises ...; or (2) benefits, financially or by receiving anything of value, from participation in a venture which has engaged in an act described in violation of paragraph (1), knowing, or, except where, in an offense under paragraph (2), the act constituting the violation of paragraph (1) is advertising, in reckless disregard of the fact, that means of force, threats of force, fraud, coercion described in subsection (e)(2), or any combination of such means will be used to cause the person to engage in a commercial sex act, or that the person has not attained the age of 18 years and will be caused to engage in a commercial sex act, shall be punished as provided in subsection (b)."

[89] Global-Tech Appliances, Inc. v. SEB S.A., 131 S.Ct. 2060, 2070 (2011)("While the Courts of Appeals articulate the doctrine of willful blindness in slightly different ways, all appear to agree on two basic requirements: (1) the defendant must subjectively believe that there is a high probability that a fact exists and (2) the defendant must take deliberate action to avoid learning of that fact"); United States v. Adorno-Molina, 774 F.3d 116, 124 (1st Cir. 2014)("A willful blindness instruction is appropriate if (1) a defendant claims a lack of knowledge, (2) the facts suggest a conscious course of deliberate ignorance, and (3) the instruction, taken as a whole, cannot be misunderstood as mandating an inference of knowledge"); United States v. Salinas, 763 F.3d 869, 878 (7th Cir. 2014)("A defendant may not escape criminal liability simply by pleading ignorance if he knows or strongly suspects he is involved in criminal dealings but deliberately avoids learning more exact information about the nature and extent of those dealings"); United States v. Mathauda, 740 F.3d 565,

568-69 (11th Cir. 2014), quoting United States v. Bisong, 384 F.3d 400 (D.C. Cir. 2011), ("We agree with the United States Court of Appeals for the District of Columbia Circuit that there are two predominant formulations of willful blindness: 'when a defendant purposely contrived to avoid learning of the facts, or the defendant was aware of a high probability of the fact in dispute and consciously avoided confirming that fact'").

[90] United States v. Anyanwu, 775 F.3d 1322, 1325 (11th Cir. 2015).

[91] United States v. Gifford, 727 F.3d 92, 98 (1st Cir. 2013)("An allegation is made with reckless disregard for the truth if the affiant in fact entertained serious doubts as to the truth of the allegations or where the circumstances evinced obvious reasons to doubt the veracity of the allegations in the application"); Betker v. Gomez, 692 F.3d 854, 860 (7th Cir. 2012)("We have said that a reckless disregard for the truth can be shown by demonstrating that the officer entertained serious doubts as to the truth of the statements, had obvious reasons to doubt their accuracy, or failed to disclose facts that he or she knew would negate probable cause"); United States v. Brown, 631 F.3d 638, 645 (3d Cir. 2011)("This definition provides two distinct ways in which conduct can be found reckless: either the affiant actually entertained serious doubts; or obvious reasons existed for him to do so, such that the finder of act can infer a subjectively reckless state of mind").

[92] 18 U.S.C. 2423(a), (b), and (c), respectively; 18 U.S.C. 2423(f).

[93] 18 U.S.C. 2423(g).

[94] H.R. 181, §8, proposed 18 U.S.C. 2423(g); H.R. 296, §11(b), proposed 18 U.S.C. 2423(g); S. 178, §11(b), proposed 18 U.S.C. 2423(g); see also H.Rept. 113-450, at 16 (2014).

[95] Syblis v. Attorney General of the U.S., 763 F.3d 348 (3d Cir. 2014), quoting, Concrete Pipe & Prods of Cal., Inc. v. Constr. Laborers Pension Trust for S. Cal., 508 U.S. 602, 622 (1993), and Schaffer ex rel. Schaffer v. Weast, 546 U.S. 49, 56 (2005)("A burden of proof by a preponderance of the evidence 'requires the trier of fact to believe that the existence of a factor is more probable than its nonexistence' ... Accordingly, the burden establishes 'which party loses if the evidence is closely balanced"); see also Siddiqui v. Holder, 670 F.3d 736, 742 (7th Cir. 2012); United States v. Manigan, 508 F.3d 621, 631 (4th 2010).

[96] Bishop v. Warden, 726 F.3d 1243, 1258 (11th Cir. 2013); United States v. Springer, 715 F.3d 535, 538 (4th Cir. 2013); Araujo v. N.J. Transit Rail Operations, Inc., 708 F.3d 152, 159 (3d Cir. 2013).

[97] S. 178, §111(a)(3), proposed 18 U.S.C. 2423(f)(3); H.R. 296, §11(a), proposed 18 U.S.C. 2423(f)(3).

[98] 18 U.S.C. 2423(b), (c), (d).

INDEX

D

E

F

G

H

I

J

L

M

N

O

P

Q

R

S